HAIDA

A Story of the Hard Fighting Tribal Class Destroyers of the Royal Canadian Navy
on the Murmansk Convoy, the English Channel, and the Bay of Biscay

WILLIAM SCLATER

Illustrated by Grant MACDONALD   *With a New Introduction by* Ted BARRIS

OXFORD
UNIVERSITY PRESS

OXFORD
UNIVERSITY PRESS

Oxford University Press is a department of the University of Oxford.
It furthers the University's objective of excellence in research, scholarship,
and education by publishing worldwide. Oxford is a registered trade mark of
Oxford University Press in the UK and in certain other countries.

Published in Canada by
Oxford University Press
8 Sampson Mews, Suite 204,
Don Mills, Ontario M3C 0H5

www.oupcanada.com

Original Edition Copyright, Canada, 1947
Material New to this Edition © Oxford University Press 2012

Library and Archives Canada Cataloguing in Publication

Sclater, William, 1907–1980
Haida : a story of the hard fighting tribal class destroyers
of the Royal Canadian Navy on the Murmansk Convoy, the
English Channel and the Bay of Biscay / William Sclater ;
introduction by Ted Barris ; illustrated by Grant Macdonald.

(The Wynford Project)
Originally published: 1946.
ISBN 978-0-19-544793-4

1. Haida (Ship). 2. World War, 1939-1945—Naval operations,
Canadian. 3. World War, 1939–1945—Personal narratives, Canadian.
4. Canada. Royal Canadian Navy—Biography. 5. Murmansk Region
(Russia)—History, Naval. 6. English Channel—History, Naval.
7. Biscay, Bay of (France and Spain)—History, Naval. I. Macdonald,
Grant, 1909–1987 II. Title. III. Series: Wynford Project

D779.C2S3 2012   940.54'5971   C2012-902403-1

Cover image: © Michael William Hrysko

Printed and bound in Canada.

1 2 3 4 — 15 14 13 12

INTRODUCTION TO THE WYNFORD EDITION

Ted Barris

On the fiftieth anniversary of Victory in Europe Day—May 8, 1995—my father, Alex Barris, and I stepped onto an open aft deck aboard HMCS *Haida*. The Second World War Tribal Class Destroyer then sat in front of Ontario Place in Toronto Harbour, where it had been moored for a quarter of a century. Alex and I welcomed media reporters, our publishing representatives, and close family members. But our special guests that midday were veterans we had invited to share the occasion with us. My father asked me to speak about the significance of the anniversary.

"I wasn't around then," I said. "But (my father) was. He was in the American Army in Czechoslovakia. And for the first time in nearly six years he knew there would probably be a tomorrow. This little ceremony is to acknowledge the role each of you played in making sure there would be a tomorrow for the rest of us."

Following our comments, we raised glasses of champagne, not just to launch our new book, *Days of Victory: Canadians Remember 1939–1945,* but to pay tribute to the men and women whose service comprised the narrative's backbone. A few moments later, contemporary crewmen aboard the only surviving Tribal Class Destroyer in the Royal Canadian Navy then invited my father and me to a nearby three-inch-fifty-calibre gun position. There we donned goggles, heavy fireproof gloves, and bibs. On command, we loaded and then fired the naval artillery piece. The sound of the exploding shell—even just a blank—startled everybody as it reverberated across the waterfront. The vibration nearly knocked the two of us over.

"Don't think we'd have made very good seamen," Dad joked.

It was quite permissible for him to say that. He'd served as a sergeant in the US Army Medical Corps in George Patton's Third Army from France to Czechoslovakia. He'd experienced his own hell in the war and had nothing to be ashamed of. I had never worn a service uniform, never served my country in the armed forces, but had written half a dozen books about those who have. The resounding blast of our ceremonial gun firing reinforced the point.

The Tribal Class Destroyer HMCS *Haida* had weathered much more fire and fury than almost any of us present that day had ever known. Commissioned in August 1943, she had performed actively in what had become, by the end of the Second World War, the third largest navy in the world. Her ship's company of about 250 officers and other ranks had served among nearly 100,000 Royal Canadian Navy wartime personnel between 1943 and 1945. She had earned battle honours from the convoy initiation ports of the western Atlantic Ocean, to the dreaded Murmansk run through the Barents Sea, and in particular, as a frontline member of the 10th Destroyer Flotilla, clearing the western flank along the D-Day invasion routes of enemy ships.

The Navy had extended her wartime service into the 1950–53 Korean War, during which her crews took up train-busting against the Communist North Korean and Chinese forces along the Yellow and Japan Seas. Then, despite an appointment at the scrap yard in 1963, the veteran destroyer had earned a second life as a tourist destination on the shores of Lake Ontario. And yet, there in Toronto Harbour on that fiftieth anniversary, amid the toasts to our book about winning the Second World War, the voices of *Haida*'s history seemed sadly silent, with only her ceremonial three-inch-fifty-cal gun giving audio postscript to a storied and illustrious role in that victory.

Now, joyously, those voices have resurfaced in a long overdue reprinting of William Sclater's *Haida: A Story of the Hard Fighting Tribal Class Destroyers of the Royal Canadian Navy on the Murmansk Convoy, the English Channel, and the Bay of Biscay.* In his original 221-page publication, first published at the war's end in 1947, Sclater stitched together the chronological tale of *Haida*'s unceremonious commissioning, her joining sister Tribals—*Athabaskan*,

Iroquois, and *Huron*—in the safe delivery of transatlantic convoys to British and Russian ports, her early tangles en route with the wolf packs of U-boats and German battleships *Scharnhorst* and *Tirpitz*, and eventually in the 10th Destroyer Flotilla ensuring successful completion of Operation Overlord on the English Channel to begin the liberation of Europe on the Normandy beaches.

Periodically, Sclater lets *Haida*'s shipmates speak, revealing the personality of a crew on task. There's the young communications rating admitting his naïveté about starshell bursts because, "This is my first ship." There are the new lyrics the crew dream up and sing to the tune of "Bless 'em all": "Bless all the seamen and gunner's mates too / Bless all the stokers and their dirty crew." And in their home-away-from-home, the British port of Plymouth, crewmen answer a gunner's satirical oratory: "What ship is always at sea on Saturdays?" he asks. "*Haida*!" they yell. And he moans "How can I pay my mess bills if I can't get to the dog races to make money?"

In particular, however, Sclater's account of pre-invasion operations on April 29, 1944, when sister ships *Haida* and *Athabaskan* chased and engaged two German Eblings (E-boats), provides among the most vivid naval encounters of the RCN at war. He takes the reader to *Haida*'s engagement with two German destroyers fleeing the scene "with a vicious burst of close-range fire," punching out one and driving the second out of control on a beach where "*Haida* let her have it, again and again, to finish her off." He then takes us back to where *Athabaskan* had sunk without a trace, leaving behind only the "eerie scene in the dim, predawn gloom. Lifejacket lights were flashing and survivors were shouting and blowing their whistles. . . . Lining the rail, *Haida*'s men encouraged them and the captain, leaning over the bridge, called them to swim in."

And if ever the picture of a gunner, a stoker, a cook, a communications hand, or a shipwrecked survivor seemed to fade from the dialogue, Sclater and his Oxford University Press publishers included in the original (and have again in the reprint) engaging ink-sketch and watercolour images strategically placed throughout the book. These are the works of navy Lieutenant Grant Macdonald, drawn from his earlier book of naval sketches entitled *Sailors*. Each telling portrait of a nameless *Haida* crewman reveals the personal insight of focus and fatigue, dedication and duty aboard a ship in the throes of war.

As Sclater points out in his author's note: "It is not in the heat and intensity of the struggle, but later in the clearer saner light of the years that come after, that the true historical perspective of men and events in times of crises may be achieved." In the context of this acknowledgment, Sclater speaks of his inspiration for writing this book, Vice Admiral George Clarence Jones, whom Sclater served under during the Second World War at a base in Atlantic Canada. (Jones, the author lamented, died before the book's publication in 1947.)

May it now be said with the return to print of *Haida* that "the true historical perspective" of this extraordinary warship and the thousands who served aboard her be reignited, like a ceremonial gun blast on an anniversary that recalled victory. *Haida* and her crews helped deliver that victory. This timeless document assures we ought not to forget.

To the people of Canada
in the homes throughout
the Dominion from whence
this ship's company came,
this book is dedicated with
respect and affection

ILLUSTRATIONS

Wherever the White Ensign flew during
the war – with the North Atlantic convoys,
on the hard reach to Murmansk, in the North
Sea, the English Channel, the Mediterranean
and the Far East – the fighting ships and
the fighting men of the Royal Canadian Navy
were well represented. For Canada's emerg-
ence as a Maritime power was a significant
and striking factor in the fight to maintain liberty and democracy.

Within the compass of these grim years,
the Great Dominion created, from small beginnings, a Navy that won the admiration of
the United Nations.

This is a book about one of the most
famous ships of that fighting Navy – H.M.
C.S. HAIDA, of the 10th Destroyer Flotilla
in the Plymouth Command. In the records
of many swift offensive forays off the
enemy-occupied coast of France, she inscrib-
ed a name that will live as long as the
White Ensign endures.

A. V. Alexander

PUBLISHER'S NOTE

Haida was first published in 1947. This facsimile edition faithfully reproduces the original text of the first edition. In the six decades since, society's attitudes toward Canada's First Nations peoples and indeed the very terms used to denote those societies have changed greatly. So have historical views of first contact between Europeans and the First Nations, relations between French and English Canada, as well as social attitudes in general toward gender and ethnicity. *Haida* is, like any creative work, an artifact of its time, and it is only fair to say that the twenty-first century reader may stumble across the occasional expression no longer in common use.

AUTHOR'S NOTE.

This is the story of a ship and her company, a Tribal Class Destroyer of the Royal Canadian Navy which, like her sisters, is a symbol of our times.

During her first commission she ranged from the gloomy wastes of the Arctic seas to the shores of Hitler-held Europe. Her guns blazed in many a fierce and spirited action as she played her part in the drama of these crucial days.

It is a book without names because to mention one would be to mention all. They, the living and the dead, prefer it so. Her company, drawn from every province in this Dominion, were common men, with little to their name. They served where one is always close to reality, in the ships which stand between us and our enemies.

They did not fight for glory or for gain. Along their decks they felt the sweep of enemy fire and saw their shipmates fall, wounded, broken and dying, but still, with grim indomitable hearts they carried on.

There is no more to say. This ship wrote her own story, and the story she wrote with her blazing guns is an imperishable chapter in the history of our people. Here is Canada.

The publisher of this book, Mr. William H. Clarke of the Oxford University Press, remarked once, in a relaxed moment, that there was one place in a book where the author could say what he pleased. This is it.

What can one say? I never wrote a book before. It is something I have always wanted to do but might never have accomplished but for the encouragement I received from the young lady who is now my wife.

For the advice and help I have received from the Navy

League of Canada I am sincerely grateful. When this book was still the rough draft of a dream, although in my ignorance I considered it practically completed, Mr. David H. Gibson, C.B.E., President of the Navy League of Canada, Mr. C. L. Burton, Major Everett Bristol, K.C., and Mr. Harry R. Gillard, together with their committee, were kind enough to have it studied, then suggested that, in their opinion, it should be submitted to the Oxford University Press.

The publishers seemed to be quite taken with the theme of the story and said they would be willing to publish it, provided I could re-write it in a manner which would make it understandable to all readers and not just those who served in the navy.

It was only then, in the latter half of 1945, that the real work of writing this book began. It has taken me more days and many more nights than I care to remember. I served in the ship throughout her actions and re-living these days and nights was not conducive to sound sleeping.

I hope I have succeeded in making it understandable to you. It has been necessary to introduce certain characters and conversation to make it so. Both characters and conversation are entirely fictitious, but the things this ship and her company accomplished are not fictitious. The operations and actions described are as accurate as words can portray them. The illustrations I was fortunate enough to have done by the well-known artist, Lieut. Grant Macdonald, whose own book of naval sketches, "Sailors", was recently published.

During part of my life I have followed the sea, in merchant ships, to the Far East, the China Coast, Indian Ocean, Mediterranean, North and South Atlantic and the Pacific. The sea knows no frontiers and the same salt combers that break on the long sands of Australia thunder into surf on the rockbound shores of Nova Scotia. Into this book I have tried to put something of the sea for it is in my mind that few of us in the inland places of this great continent realize how much the sea affects our daily lives.

It was not to the incidence of chance but to the existence of a great and friendly seapower that Canada has owed her beginnings as a nation. That truth was never more strikingly portrayed than in the recent hostilities, when all our future was dependent upon the maintenance of our seaborne communications. The same truth holds good today in times of peace as in war. Canada is a trading nation, completely dependent upon her exports for the comfort and well-being of her people, and it is upon the freedom of the seas that we must always rely.

The man who first gave me the inspiration to write this book was a senior officer of the Royal Canadian Navy. It had been my fortune earlier in the war, to have served on his staff at an Atlantic Base. I picked up a lot of "buzzes" on him before reporting there. As usual I found about ninety per cent of the "buzz" completely unfounded though, in our early days, we moved with no small amount of trepidation when in his vicinity because of it. The first time he sent for me, between my own consciousness of my sins of omission and the "buzzes" I had heard, my impulse was to start running the other way.

His job was a big one, befitting the man. Through his hands were pouring the rough, unfinished drafts of men for service in the Battle of the Atlantic and the hastily-built ships from the building yards of the Dominion. Crews had to be trained and put into operational duty at sea. New bases had to be planned, organized and manned, with all the specialists, technicians and other personnel required to direct, operate and service the diversity of functional activity and multitudinous equipment that comprise a modern naval base.

Over and beyond these matters were the strategy and tactics to be devised and used to combat the U-boats and hold open the sea lanes; the direction of the merchant ship convoys and a hundred other matters on high levels that came under his personal direction. One could understand and forgive a man with these matters in his hands, if his time was too fully occupied for those under his command to know him, except as a somewhat nebulous figure in the background. With the nation fighting for its very existence, and the fighting very much in his theatre of operations, he had little time to give to visiting.

He was a seaman. One look at him made that obvious. His weatherbeaten countenance had been marked and tanned by the winds and waters of the seven seas. His look was keen and direct and he wasted no time in coming to the point. As a young officer in the last war he had fought in the North Atlantic and North Sea and risen later to his first command of a destroyer. In the years between the wars, ashore and afloat he had met the exacting demands required by the naval service of those who win promotion, and worked his way steadily up that difficult ladder. As we came to know him we found him to be a richly human individual, with a quick appreciation and understanding of the difficulties which we brought to him for solution. In all our meetings we never left without having been given a constructive thought and a fresh inspiration for our duties.

Intensely practical, as befits a seaman, he knew, none better, the rough untrainedness of the human material that was his to direct and control. He did not seek to make them supermen. All he asked of any man was that he do his best within the compass of his abilities and he stood behind his men. He took what was to hand in men, ships and equipment and made it do.

Publicity was something he never sought, nor wanted for himself. He was keenly aware of its value however, for keeping the nation informed and for its vital importance as a factor in service morale. The praise or plaudits that came his way he gave to those who served under him.

Completely unassuming, he refused to accept any personal privileges for himself or his family through his high office. I have travelled with him when, dressed in civilian clothes, he would take his turn in the queue on a crowded train and wait patiently for more than an hour for a seat in the diner. He asked nothing that was not available in the ordinary way to any private citizen.

Few beyond his immediate staff saw much of him or realized the wide extent of his activities in these busy, bustling days of war. Those who would have made much of it he brushed off with his disarming smile. He would be the first to disclaim it, yet it is to him, more than any other officer in the service, that the thanks of the nation are due for the navy that came into being in these fateful days.

In the officers who served close to him he inspired a personal affection and regard of the highest order. I know I count it the greatest privilege I have ever known to have served under this man.

He was a Nova Scotian, a big, broad-shouldered son of that province which is our Atlantic bastion and which has done so much to enrich both our heritage and the annals of the sea. He had an inherited love for salt water and it is in my mind that the ship of which this book is written exemplifies his character in many ways. The bold, invigorating dash which made her famous, her swift effectiveness and reliability were counterparts of his nature. He would have loved to sail in her. The fact that her Captain was his own trusted Chief of Staff both before and after was a constant source of pride and satisfaction to him.

It is not in the heat and intensity of the struggle, but later in the clearer saner light of the years that come after, that the true historical perspective of men and events in times of crisis may be achieved. When that day comes Canada will know how much she owes to this gentleman of the Royal Canadian Navy who served her so well.

He will not be here to receive that acclaim, or shrug it off as was his wont and give the credit to the navy that he loved so well. On a sunlit winter afternoon in February of 1946, he came home to Halifax for the last time, to be buried with full naval honours in a grave on a gentle hillside looking seaward over the great base and harbour that was his pride and joy. Struck down suddenly at the peak of his career, just when the long battle he had fought so well had been won so decisively, he did not live to reap its fruits.

He shall not be forgotten. He lives always in the hearts of those who knew him, in the fighting ships which defend our cause, in the men and women who wear the blue uniform of the naval service. This book was written at his suggestion. It is his book, written for him, for Vice Admiral George Clarence Jones, C.B., R.C.N., Chief of Naval Staff of the Royal Canadian Navy, a great Admiral and a great gentleman. It has been a privilege to write it.

WILLIAM SCLATER

Toronto, Ontario,
October, 1946.

HAIDA

HAIDA

CHAPTER I

The Commissioning was a brief and simple affair. At the command they came to attention. They offed caps. There was a prayer, a dedication and a few quiet words from the Captain.

No bands or bugles played, just the simple words while the new destroyer lay alongside the dock in the shadow of the high derricks of the building yard. Down wind drifted the staccato noise of rivetting hammers from other fighting craft under construction but here, for this moment, there was a hush.

Overlooking the long maindeck and the ranks of seamen drawn up amidships for the ceremony were the "mateys" who had built her, the men and women of this big, sprawling British wartime shipyard. Clustered on top of old gun mounts, boilers and other vantage points along the dockside they watched the final end of their labours, the official taking over by the new Royal Canadian naval crew which had arrived that morning and the initial naval procedure, the commissioning ceremony.

For them this August afternoon of 1943 was the culmination of more than two years of labour. This new destroyer was their product, the creation of their brains and their hands. Her building time had been a grim chapter in their history. Throughout the long months in which she had come from a mass of blueprints on the drawing boards to a finished, lethal weapon of war, they had faced the death and destruction which rode the night skies. They had seen the dawn break over homes reduced to rubble and looked upon the death and disablement that lay in the wake of the bombers. But through it all they had carried on, fighting back in the only way they knew. This was it.

3

Into this long ship's building they had put the vengeful-
ness of their own dour angered spirit. In her grim guns and
speedy hull were bitter memories of the ravages they had
known. To them she was an instrument of vengeance,
something which could strike back with power and force.

Though they could not hear what was being said, they
could see the Captain standing by the ship's bell as he
addressed the crew. As they watched they saw him take off
his cap and wave it in the air, and then they heard the sailors
cheering, three times and then a tiger.

Recognizing it as a salute to their labours they cheered
back with hoarse shouts of "Good luck, boys!" and "Get one
for us!" Some of the women workers cheered frantically
and then cried, dabbing at their eyes with the edges of the
coloured handkerchiefs they wore on their heads.

They still watched as the long lines of seamen stiffened
at a low-voiced command. There was a momentary pause
and then, at another command, the blue-clad ranks from
Canada turned and dismissed. The new destroyer was in
commission.

Reluctantly then the mateys left their vantage points and
dispersed to other tasks. This new "lady" they had created
from steel and iron was theirs no longer. She belonged now
to the strong young hands of the navy crew which had taken
her over, another unit of the mighty fleet of growing Allied
sea-power. Yet, in another, wider sense, they knew that she
would still be theirs, operated for and on their behalf, fighting in the great cause of human freedom. With that they
were content.

Aboard the ship the new crew were granted a "make and
mend", as soon as they were dismissed following the commissioning ceremony, to settle their gear in and look over
their new home.

They were a mixed lot from the viewpoint of experience.

4

Quite a number, particularly among the petty officers, gunners and torpedomen, were men of the permanent navy who had joined long before the outbreak of war and had been widely experienced both before and since, veterans of the evacuation from France, the Norway show and the "Med." The majority, however, were men of the R.C.N.V.R., the volunteer citizen sailors who had joined for the duration.

For the most part they were graduates of the corvettes, frigates and destroyers of the North Atlantic Escort Forces, the guardians of the merchant fleets which, through long days and longer nights, from Halifax to "Newfie", Reykjavik and 'Derry, had fought the U-boats on the wide reaches of the North Atlantic.

The chance of war, in drafts from manning bases, courses and other ships had brought them here. This new ship was theirs. Old hands and new, permanent force or duration only, this was one thing they had in common. In her they would live and in her they would fight. She would be their home, for some the last home on earth they would ever know.

They were all Canadians: men from the schools, offices, farms and factories of Ontario, Quebec and the West, men from the mines and lumber camps, from the ships and fishing craft of the Maritimes and British Columbia. Their average age was twenty-five.

Most of them had come to the sea through war but deep within them they looked upon it as an older heritage to which they had returned, a heritage to which their youth and their instincts responded well. To the veterans the newer hands were welcome additions. They took their places naturally, pooling their experience so that each became part of a common entity, a new ship's company, while retaining the independence and individuality that is the characteristic of those who go down to the sea in ships.

This new ship was the first Tribal Class Destroyer most

5

of them had ever seen and they studied her with critical, appraising eyes. Like a man who had bought a car, sight unseen, they wondered just what they'd bought. There had been "buzzes", and in the navy the "buzz" is the most unreliable form of rumour known.

Tribals, according to the buzz, were obsolete, slow and undergunned. Apart from the *Cossack* they had heard little of them in this war and the disheartening comment of one old hand was a brief "They all get sunk!" It was not without truth. Of the sixteen originally built by the Royal Navy, only four remained afloat. The "price of admiralty" had come high in these crucial years.

Despite the buzzes, they found the beginning of a profound satisfaction and secret pride as they looked her over. She appeared to be roomy forward, compared with escort destroyers, though seamen's and stoker's messdecks were not roomy actually when the number of hands who had to live there was tallied. Fighting destroyers in modern war give first place to equipment. The various messes were fitted in the usual "stripped for action" pattern. There was little beyond the bare necessities.

If living room was restricted she made up for it in equipment. New gadgets of every description had been fitted in every spare corner. She was obviously built for just one purpose and that was to fight. For that purpose she was unsurpassed.

"Boy, look at these guns," said an anti-submarine or "Asdic" rating to his mate, as they inspected the high, built-up foredeck behind the knifelike bows, pointing to the forward gun mountings.

There were twin gun barrels projecting forward from each of the two turrets on the foresection. One mounting was on the foredeck itself, the other was stepped above and behind it, being built on top of the foredeck housing. Behind and

6

above them both loomed the high fighting bridge, open to the skies, with only a low glass windshield to shield the bridge crew from wind and weather.

"Wonder what they are. They look big enough to be five inchers," he added.

A seaman gunner standing in silent contemplation of the two gun turrets enlightened him. "These are twin four-point-sevens," he said, "one of the best mountings ever made."

"Where does the ammunition come up?" asked the submarine detection man as he looked around the bare gundeck.

"See these little hatches on the deck there," explained the gunner; "the shells come up on automatic hoists, right up through the messdecks. The magazines are away down below in the bottom of the ship."

"How do they fire them?"

"Everything's automatic on this ship. These guns are operated from a central control point; everything is calculated there by machines and they are ranged, fired, corrected, ranged and fired again and again."

"Don't they have a gun crew?"

The gunner regarded them with amusement. "Where have you fellows been all your lives?" he asked, but there was no insult in the remark. "Sure they have a gun crew. Somebody's got to load 'em, check the range, keep 'em on target and all that. You just get on a supply party some time and find out what it means to feed the shells to a pair of babies like these."

"She sure has plenty guns," remarked the anti-submarine man.

"There's another two turrets down aft. The one on the quarterdeck is a twin four-point-seven like these. The one above it on the afterdeck housing is a four-inch high angle."

"That's for anti-aircraft, isn't it?"

7

"That's for anything," said the gunner. "The twin four-inch barrels can be elevated to fight off planes, dive bombers or anything up top. They can also be depressed for submarines, E-boats or anything on the surface. It's a useful turret that."

"She's got a lot more guns than a River Class destroyer like the convoy escorts," remarked the anti-submarine man's mate.

"I'll say she has," replied the gunner. "She's got seven times the firepower of an ordinary destroyer at least, maybe more. She's really a pocket cruiser."

The pipe of "hands to supper" brought the tours of inspection to an end. The shank of the afternoon had passed swiftly and it was time to eat. The messmen whose turn it was to carry the food from the galley to the individual messes were hauling the supper. It was roast beef, roasted potatoes, beans, rice pudding and coffee. As they ate at their tables in the messdecks, the men discussed their ship.

She was nothing to write home about for comfort or facilities. On that they were all agreed, but her fighting equipment was something that brought a light to their eyes. She had the stuff they needed and wanted, and plenty of it. In this ship they felt they could tackle almost anything.

"Pardon my ignorance," asked a young seaman, "but what *is* a Tribal destroyer? I've heard reasons but, on the level, why do they call them Tribals?"

"It's a class," replied a "Killick", as a Leading Seaman is known in the lower deck vernacular. "There's River Class, like the escort destroyers; Hunt Class, that's these little fellows; Javelin Class, they're the ones with all the torpedo tubes; and so on. The Tribals are really an outclass in destroyers. They are all given Tribal names. The R.N. call theirs after all kinds of tribes, like Tartar, Ashanti,

8

CHANNEL

Grant Macdonald
RCNVR 1945

"THE COMMANDING OFFICER WAS ALWAYS A SUBJECT OF
    INTEREST."

Cossack, and Afridi. We call ours after Indian tribes like Athabaskan, Iroquois, Huron and so on."

Down in the Stoker's Mess the conversation was mostly on speed and pressures. The "Old Man" had "spliced the mainbrace" in traditional fashion. All hands had received an extra tot of grog, as the mixed rum and water daily issue is known, and the stokers were feeling good. The engine and boiler rooms had met with their approval. They'd be cool and they figured she'd be fast enough to suit everybody.

In the Chief's and P.O.'s Mess, where the Coxswain, the Chief Gunner's Mate, the Torpedo Gunner's Mate, the Chief Engine Room Artificer and other senior ratings were gathered, the talk was mostly of ships and men.

"What's the Old Man like?" asked one. "I never sailed with him before, though I've heard about him." The Commanding Officer who ruled their destinies was always a subject of interest.

"Oh, he knows his stuff," returned another. "He's strict and God help the man who doesn't know his stuff, but he's fair. He was brought up in the old school. He's a destroyer man."

"I was with him in the St. Laurent," interjected another. "He was in command of her during the evacuation from France. He can sure handle a ship."

"The old Sally Rand," said the first speaker, alluding to the *St. Laurent* by her navy nickname, "didn't she pull off a big rescue job in the North Atlantic, a big British liner carrying a bunch of German and Italian prisoners when she was torpedoed by a German submarine? That was the Arandora Star, wasn't it? She was torpedoed with all these prisoners on board."

"Yeh, that was after France fell. We were on convoy duty on the North Atlantic then. This Old Man was still in command. That was a funny one, all these Krauts and

9

Eyeties hollering for help after one of their own U-boats had got them. A RAF plane came over and we signalled and told her what had happened. She signalled back, 'How bloody funny! ' "

"The Gunner T on this packet was in the French show too, wasn't he?"

"Yeh, but he was in a British destroyer then. They took the British Expeditionary Force to France. He was torpedoed in the old Ottawa afterwards."

"What's the wardroom crowd like?"

"We got quite a bunch, eighteen officers all told, mostly V.R.'s, with corvette experience."

"Well, what do you think of her, Happy?" asked the Cox'n interrupting the reminiscences to query a cheerful looking P.O. at the end of the table.

"Me? I'm a Communist," answered Happy, "but I'll let the dice talk."

Solemnly he extracted a pair of crap dice from his trouser pocket and rolled them on the table.

"A natch!" ejaculated the men beside him as the dice rolled and stopped, showing a four and a three uppermost.

"I agree," said Happy, "she's a good ship, she'll be a natural all right."

In the wardroom, where the officers and guests for the cocktail party which followed the commissioning had gathered, the dockyard superintendent was proposing a toast.

She had been named, a name that was strange and fierce but yet had music in it, the name of an Indian tribe which made its home on the rocky, seagirt Charlottes off the British Columbia coast. A bold seafaring people, these island Indians built their totem poles of stone. There was nothing soft about them or the ship which bore their name. The new destroyer had been called H.M.C.S. Haida.

Raising his glass the stocky superintendent gave his toast. "To H.M.C.S. Haida," he said, "and to every man who sails in her. Good luck and good hunting!"

They drank to that, each man with a quietly-spoken "Good luck" as he emptied his glass.

They liked their new ship. She was well-built and they felt she was well-manned. It was a big crew, upwards of two hundred and fifty fighting men. A ship like this needed a big crew and there were many specialists, specially-trained men to operate the multitudinous gadgets for submarine detection, to handle the power-operated gun turrets, the power-operated torpedo tubes and the special gear for many significant purposes.

Viewed in silhouette she was an inspiring sight to any man used to small ships, as most of them were. The long barrels of the twin four-point-sevens pointing ominously ahead were impressive behind the high, rakish bows.

Well-proportioned, she was bigger than she seemed, running to more than three hundred and seventy feet in length, yet her beam of thirty-seven feet was wide enough to make her comfortable in a seaway.

Steel ladders on either side led down from the high foredeck to the long maindeck which extended right to the stern. The steel lattice mast was right behind the bridge and amidships were the two flat oval-shaped funnels. At each side of the ship, protected by the break from the high foredeck, were the seaboats, a slim whaler and a 26-foot motor cutter on the starboard side, both slung on davits, and a similar cutter on the port side. In addition, a small "skimmer" motorboat was secured on deck on the port side.

Between the two funnels a narrow gangway across the ship, about eight feet above the maindeck, supported the second battery of twin Oerlikon guns. These were machine guns capable of being used for anti-aircraft or surface firing.

11

There was a twin gun-mounting on each side of the gangway. Similar mountings were located on each side of the bridge superstructure and another pair on each side of the afterdeck housing.

There were four torpedo tubes, quadruple mountings. These were on the maindeck amidships, behind the second funnel. Power-operated, they all moved together and could be fired over either side at any angle desired.

The engine room was below the maindeck. It was a compact power unit. Three Admiralty drum-type oil-fuelled boilers supplied the steam for the turbines. These, rated at forty-four thousand horsepower, drove the shafts which turned the big twin propellers for a designed speed of thirty-six knots. This was the domain of the Engineer Officer, a Lieutenant of the R.C.N., his assistant, an R.C.N.V.R. Lieutenant, and the E.R.A.'s and Stokers, each non-commissioned group under a Chief Petty Officer.

Behind this was the one-storey afterdeck housing in which was the Sick Bay, with its two berths; the Commanding Officer's day cabin, which he used only in harbour; officers' washrooms and storage rooms. A passageway led through the centre of this housing in which were hatches leading down to officers' quarters, ship's office and ammunition magazines.

On the deck which roofed this housing were mounted the twin four-inch high angle guns known as X mounting. Up here also was the big searchlight, the after emergency bridge and the multiple-barreled pom-pom gun used for anti-aircraft or close-range surface duty.

Down aft, on the quarterdeck, as the stern-section of the maindeck is known, was the twin four-point-seven mounting known as Y gun, its gunners shielded from the blast of X gun barrels above them by a flash screen which was really an after extension of the steel deck on which X gun was mounted. The two forward turrets were known as A and B.

Down aft too were the depth charge throwers and racks of depth charges ready to be dropped overboard.

The new ship, although her crew were aboard and she had been completely fitted out, was not yet ready for sea duty. Between her and that desirable state of efficiency known as "being in all respects ready for war" was the period known as "working up".

The working up programme, or "Wups", as the service describes this period, is a time of trying and testing. During it the ship's company is required to handle the ship and her equipment in every conceivable form of operational evolution which may be required of them in service. It is a miniature preview of everything that may be expected to happen.

It was a busy time for all hands and they were glad when the lean-faced Captain and the brusquely cherubic First Lieutenant finally intimated they were beginning to look and act like sailors again and that a few more months, or years, might hold some hope. "Wups" was over now and the ship was ready to proceed to her first operational base.

Her crew were ready, too. The leaven of the old had worked in well with the new and the ship's company were settling into one entity with their ship. The North Atlantic hands had absorbed the experience of the veterans of the evacuation from France, the Norwegian campaign and the Mediterranean convoys. They had absorbed, too, the atmosphere and the spirit of the people ashore, the people of the blitzed buildings and the friendly pubs. They were eager to get going.

CHAPTER II

Being in all respects ready for war H.M.C.S. Haida will sail at 0800 to pass seagate at 0820 and proceed to join units of the X destroyer flotilla as directed in my 214324.

Scapa Flow presented an inspiring panoply of naval might as the trim new destroyer came through the seagate and steamed up to her anchorage on a brisk October morning. Here were the "big fellows", the great battleships and aircraft carriers of the Home Fleet, together with their attendant cruisers, destroyers and auxiliaries. With them too were fighting ships of the United States, France, Norway and several other countries. The "Flow" was home to thousands of men and hundreds of fighting ships.

Shorewards it was a grim, bleak prospect. The Orkney Islands, where the great British base is situated, are Northeast of the Scottish mainland, far enough North to be almost beyond the treeline in a latitude similar to Hudson.Bay. The nearest town is Kirkwall, a small town with a limited population and few amenities. The splendid harbour itself is bounded by low, rocky islands; lands of peat, moss and low hills. Looking at this the seamen from Canada felt they understood where the Scots acquire some of their more rugged characteristics.

On the bridge the signalmen were kept busy as the new Tribal steamed in. Signal lamps were blinking out messages of welcome. "Hello, Canada, glad to have you with us" and many other greetings were flashed. Here too were old shipmates, for two of the lean Tribals whose lamps were flashing invitations were ships from home, H.M.C.S. Iroquois and H.M.C.S. Huron.

There was a joyful reunion and exchange of news when the crews got together. *Iroquois* had been in action against

14

"SIGNAL LAMPS WERE BLINKING WELCOME."

enemy planes and had shot one down. *Huron* had been busily engaged in a variety of duties since her arrival a few weeks before. The only missing member was H.M.C.S. Athabaskan, refitting in a dockyard port after being hit by a glider bomb in the Bay of Biscay and not due to arrive for several weeks yet.

The few days here passed all too swiftly. There was much to do. Minor deficiencies spotted during the workup had to be made good and provision and handling of supplies of all kinds had to be arranged. There was shore leave, but only the most ambitious spirits ventured to land.

Liberty boats were available, picking up liberty men, as shore-bound sailors on leave are called, at regular hours, but from the destroyer anchorage it was a long way in. Then, too, there is nearly always a fresh breeze in Scapa, except when it blows a full gale, and the trip was long, sprayswept and discouraging. All leave ceased at 6.30 p.m. so that before one was properly ashore it was time to go back. There was also, and this was important, nothing to do when one did get ashore.

The base, however, was well-organized. Supplies, mail and movies were always right on hand. There was much intership visiting and the ship's company were learning to like living "at home".

As the last adjustments were made and the ship supplied and fuelled for sea, a new flood of buzzes was loosed as to where she would be bound. Some had it she was escorting a battleship to the Med, and then getting into the Italian business. Others anticipated an imminent invasion of Norway. There was also a whisper about "the Pacific". It was a very secret buzz that last one, right from an ordinary seaman's whiskers.

When the signal finally did arrive and became known, the sunshine buzzes about Pacific isles full of beaches with languorous, lovelorn maidens took quite a beating. It was a rude and chilly truth. Operational, the new destroyer's job was with her sister ships. She was bound "down North".

The news gave the ship's company quite a jolt. In this part of the world "down North" meant mainly one thing, the far-famed Murmansk convoy. Not a man aboard had missed hearing some yarn about that run. In lower deck messes and in the wardroom that night they listened avidly to each other's stories about the "toughest passage of them all", fascinated by the thought that they, too, were going to be on it.

Even the N.R. (Naval Reservist) Leading Hand in the seaman's mess, a usually silent Bluenose fisherman from Nova Scotia was moved to speech. "My cousin, he's an N.R. Lieutenant in command of a trawler, was on that run. He said it was bloody. He organized the ship's company into three watches, one to fight off air attack, one to fight off submarine attack and one to deal with surface attack. That way he hoped some of them would be able to get some sleep for some of the time, anyway. He was wrong.

"They got the whole bloody works at one time. The Luftwaffe came over in force, a hundred and fifty bombers, and they sank nearly the whole leading line of the convoy in the first attack. Surface craft were sighted and then the U-boats came in. The convoy was broken up and ordered to disperse. He took two of the merchant ships up into the ice. They were there for two weeks and they had to paint the ships white to escape detection."

"Yeah," said a seaman, "remember the Cornet, that big Liberty ship that got bashed up South of Newfie and was eight months getting fixed up in the U.K. She was bound for Murmansk. I was talking to one of her guys when she got back to New York. He said they went so far North they were going through lanes in the ice. A tanker got hit

16

ahead of them and they had to wait until she sank to get through. The ship behind them was hit too. They got to Russia and had just unloaded and pulled out into the stream when the Krauts came over and bombed the docks. They got the whole damn cargo. Twelve months to get there, then Bimbo!"

"They were the guys who said they hailed a boatload of survivors off the North Cape and told them to come alongside and be picked up," interjected another. "The bloke in the boat just looked at them an' said, 'No bloody fear. We've had ours. You go ahead an' get yours.'"

Even *Haida's* uncommunicative signalmen were garrulous this night. Up in the signal office beneath the bridge the Yeoman was telling a yarn about a British Admiral who signalled a German plane. "Old 'Steamboat' got fed up," he told the listening duty signalmen. "This German plane had been circling round the convoy for hours, just out of range, shadowing them. His neck was sore from keeping turning round to watch him and the ack-ack (anti-aircraft) guncrews were dizzy keeping him covered all the time in case he came in.

"'Make a signal to that plane, Yeoman," says Steamboat. 'Give him my compliments and ask him if he'll circle the other way for a change and give our necks a rest.' The Yeoman made it in plain language. The Kraut acknowledged and turned the other way. His neck must've been sore too."

Down aft in the Wardroom the occupants looked up in surprise as the Navigating Officer hustled in with his coat collar turned up and showing signs of great pseudo-agitation.

"A rum please, steward," he said. "No! Make it a double rum and put plenty of rum in it."

"Just heard the news," he explained apologetically to the interested spectators. "Murmansk. . . . . Brrrrr!" Accept-

17

ing the drink from the white-coated steward, he raised a shaking arm and gulped some.

"Might as well fill up with anti-freeze now. You'll get cold tummies before you get to Murmansk," he admonished a couple of open-mouthed junior officers. Downing the drink and muttering something about six sheepskins, he made for the dining table and sat down. "Two of everything, steward," he said. "Now that I'm working for Uncle Joe I gotta eat good. If only my aged mother could see me now. She was born in the Welsh coalfields and was always a Red," he explained. With that he fell silent and went to work on his soup.

Actually the Murmansk convoy setup had changed vastly since it was first undertaken. Sea and air escorts had been steadily developed and the situation in the Northern seas had shown consistent improvement as a result. The hazards, for all that, were still heavy. Shadowing aircraft and U-boats attempted to keep tab on convoy movements, and there was always the possibility of attack by large German surface craft known to be based in Norwegian waters.

Forces for the multitudinous operations in these areas were provided from the big base at Scapa Flow. This was the nerve centre of the command of the seas controlling the approaches to the island kingdom from North, East and West.

Through the high latitudes from Iceland and the Americas, and up and around the North Cape to Russia, big convoys were moving regularly in their slow, impressive formations. To these, among other operations, *Haida* and her sister Tribals were to give their supporting strength.

Next morning they slipped from their buoys and sailed out of Scapa, steaming swiftly to the Northward to rendezvous with their convoy. Finding it on arriving at the given position they proceeded to take up their escort stations.

To most of them, the sight of the long lines of merchant

ships, loaded to their Plimsoll marks with stores of war, brought familiar memories. In their previous ships, the escort destroyers, frigates, corvettes and minesweepers of the North Atlantic Escort Forces, they had often accompanied similar convoys from New York, Boston, Halifax and Sydney on the North Atlantic crossing.

Here, on the other side of the Atlantic, they were meeting them now as Murmansk Escort Forces, the guardians of the final grim leg of the long voyage. To the convoy, *Haida* and her sisters were the symbols of the last hard lap but to the seamen in the Tribals the convoy was a link with the ports from which it had come, the ports of North America which they had known so well.

Taking up their escort stations and slowing down to accommodate their patrols to convoy speed, they looked it over. There is always something inexpressibly majestic about a convoy at sea. Like a proud, widespread phalanx, the merchant ships maintain their slow and stately way, their holds packed with the products of the armament plants of North America and Great Britain.

Guns, tanks, shells, locomotives, trucks and medical supplies; even their decks were piled with the paraphernalia of war. Among the tanks, trucks and locomotives could be seen the black painted bodies of planes, the crated wings beside them. Big tankers, carrying the vital oil and gas, on which all movement of ships, planes and armies is dependent in modern warfare, were steaming in the inside lanes, shielded to some extent from U-boat attack by the outer lines of ships.

All this great body of ships and men was moving slowly and steadily across the roof of the world up here in the Arctic seas; the big protected cargoes destined to play their part in the turning tide of battle on the snow-covered plains of Russia as the invaders retreated sullenly from Stalingrad.

19

It brought home to the watching seamen the hard fact that war knows no frontiers, only friends and enemies.

Each mile to the Northward was another mile made good on the long passage but it took them just that much farther into the darkness. Inexorably the period of daylight shortened until the only sign of noon was a feeble flicker on the Southern horizon.

Time ceased to have much meaning. They knew when they had left Scapa . . . they knew that they would arrive at Murmansk when they got there, if they did. Surprisingly, it was not nearly as cold as they had anticipated, not nearly as cold as it would be on the winter passage between Halifax and Newfoundland. The long arm of the Gulf Stream which kept this sea route open prevented the extremes of sub-zero temperatures that would otherwise have been inevitable. There were other discomforts in place of cold. Mist and fog, added to the gloomy twilight in which they sailed made visibility a doubtful quantity much of the time and there was a raw dampness in the atmosphere which they did not care for at all.

The Northern Lights traversed the sky at times in all their majesty but in an area which made some startled seamen realize for the first time just how far North the ships really were. Red, a cheerful tow-headed gunner from Ontario, looked at this phenomenon in silence for a time and then voiced his unbelief to the guncrew on Y gun where he was stationed.

"If these are the Northern Lights, how come they're in the wrong direction?" he asked.

The big Bluenose Leading Hand, who had served in whalers in the Arctic, grinned quietly in the darkness. "Maybe you'll believe me now, Red. I told you we were away North. We're so far North that the Northern Lights are due South of us."

20

"Oh boy, wait till I get back to Toronto," said Red, "won't I have something to tell the gang now."

It seemed almost incredible that U-boats would be operating away up here in these gloomy wastes of seas but neither the Captains of the escort nor the Masters of the convoy harboured any illusions.

They knew that astern of them, following them day and night like prowling jackals, were the submarines of the enemy. Woe betide any ship unfortunate enough to be in collision here or suffer a breakdown that would cause her to lag astern. It was true that the U-boats were chary of direct attacks. The German submarine crews knew the strength of the escort and had no more desire to perish in these freezing waters than the men of the convoy. Stragglers however were something else again.

Shepherding their charges like sheepdogs bringing along a flock of sheep, the fighting ships kept the convoy in formation and were quick to check on any ship dropping out of position. It was not an easy task in the limited visibility and anti-submarine watches were maintained at full strength day and night, the earphoned operators listening intently for the sounds that would betray the presence of the hated enemy.

Aboard *Haida* it was warm and comfortable below decks. Heat was provided by both hot water radiators and small electric heaters. The only drawback was that the constant blackout necessitated all portholes being kept closed and the air below decks got pretty thick at times, compounding the odour of wet oilskins, drying clothes, food and tobacco into the indescribable "fug" found only in ships at sea but which, to most sailors, is almost unnoticeable.

It was into this atmosphere that the Starboard Watch trooped one midnight on being relieved by the Port Watch.

21

The men from Y gun were among them and Red, feeling cheerful, broke into song.

"Oh what a beautiful morning, oh what a beautiful day," he warbled blithely.

"There goes the first one," said the Killick.

"It's the first sign all right," agreed a gunner. "When they start singing to themselves, it's really bad."

"Just about as bad as his singing," returned the Killick as he tossed a seaboot at Red and ordered him to pipe down and turn in. "You can sing when we get to Russia, if we don't throw you overboard before that," he added.

They stripped off their heavy seagear; oilskins, sheepskins, duffle coats and helmets were tossed down on deck. One or two helped themselves to a cup of "Kye", from the left behind pot of the nourishing chocolate cocoa which had been made for the departed Port Watch. For the most part, they sought immediate refuge in sleep, huddled in blankets on the lockers or in hammocks.

The dim light from the shaded bulbs was left on and they slept heavily in the thick atmosphere. An hour passed, and there was little movement among the recumbent figures. Here a man slept with his seabooted foot hanging over the side of his hammock; over on a locker seat another lay full length, face down. They were a long way from home and the comforts they once had known.

Then suddenly, deep into their consciousness penetrated the insistent buzzing of the Action Stations alarm, sounding the warning tocsin that might mean that almost anything had happened. None knew better than these men how swiftly disaster can strike. The sleepers came to their feet hastily. Some grabbed a pair of boots or a duffle coat as they ran, but most of them went as they were. This was it.

Pushing aside the two layers of heavy canvas blackout curtains across the hatchways that led outside, they hurried out into the dark dampness of the maindeck. Here the stream divided as the men ran to their different stations. Now and then a couple going in opposite directions collided and there would be a muttered curse as they separated and carried on. No one had time to waste. Every second counted now.

Within seconds, a steady stream of reports was reaching the bridge as each station was fully manned. At the gun turrets the Port Watch crew members grinned wryly as their sleepy-eyed mates filled up their ranks.

"What's doing?" asked Red as he fastened the chinstrap on his ear muffler.

"Submarine alarm," replied another. "It looks like they got one on the other side of the convoy. We heard the explosion and then the balloon went up. They're depth-charging over there now."

They waited, alert and ready, but nothing developed in their sector, and half an hour later the "Secure Action Stations" was piped and the tired Starboard Watch went below again. Some of them lay down "all standing", sleeping as they were. Within minutes they were fast asleep. At four o'clock in the morning they would have to relieve the Port Watch and spend the next four hours at stations. Sleep was the only thing that mattered now.

In the morning, they heard the news. A U-boat had slipped in a lucky torpedo and got one of the merchant ships. Most of the crew had been picked up by a rescue ship and the marauder was still being hunted. That was the first one. In the messdecks they wondered who'd be next.

Two days later a plane was sighted momentarily, low down on the Southern horizon as they rounded North Cape far to seaward. There was no identification. It might have been one of the enemy's on reconnaissance or it might

23

have been British, but no chances were taken. Precautionary measures went into effect at once.

And that was all. Tense and expectant, the crew found themselves watching, almost disappointed, as they entered the approaches to Russia and a destroyer closed the convoy and accompanied them in. There was no stop-over in the land of the Soviets. After refuelling they turned around and came back to Britain with a convoy of ships in ballast.

It was another quick turnaround again when they got back to Scapa. Ships were short and they were needed, so it was refuel, revictual and sail back again to the wastes of the Northern seas, back to the dim grey leaden water, the mists, the fogs and the darkness. And in the weeks that followed they repeated the same old endless story, always leaving the land as soon as they got there for the lonely, silent reaches once again.

One good thing about it was that they were getting to know each other. The monotony had turned their thoughts towards themselves and they were finding out what manner of men were the shipmates who sailed with them.

There were characters like the balding, bulging, cheerful Chief Petty Officer, the Cox'n, who owned to thirty-five years of age "and not a day more". He was a vigorous and able individual even if he remembered incidents of bygone navy days that happened while he was still in school, if he was only thirty-five, and they accepted him with the lenience that is the prerogative of experience.

There was a Torpedo Gunner's Mate, a big man hewn of the rock of the salt seas who knew the seaports of the world as he knew his own hand. Quiet-spoken, his new mates knew little of him until they heard him yarning one night in the mess with two of his kin, old hands of the regular service.

The talk ranged far and wide. They heard of Eddie's Café on the China Coast, of the time the Red Marines left

24

"THE TALK RANGED FAR AND WIDE."

their beer and Eddie Miller, "middleweight champ of the China Fleet he was then" taught some smart guys a needed lesson. There was the China girl who was the cause of a Petty Officer going adrift from one of the destroyers in the China Fleet.

"Three days he was away an' when he comes back he has a yarn a mile long. Says he was slugged on the Nanking Road and just came to 'alf an hour ago. He looked it, too. 'Buster' was the Old Man on that packet; he's a Rear Admiral in Newfie now and one of the best men they got in this navy. He give him plenty. The P.O. never said a word for a long time but one night I seen him looking at a picture. 'She was worth it, boy,' he says to me, 'a man's only young once.'"

They heard of the dance hall in Singapore, where the floor was made of mirrors with ventilating grates between them through which the breeze blew up; of Pompey and Davenport; of summer cruises to the Baltic and the Riviera; of Rio, Sydney, Valparaiso and Callao; of Halifax, Montreal and Esquimalt.

One of the officers aboard had been torpedoed and sunk three times in this war already, they discovered. The Gunner T was a survivor of the destroyer *Ottawa* when she was torpedoed and lost one night in the North Atlantic. "He really went through it there," was the way the Torpedo Gunner's Mate put it. He had heard the yarn from a fellow who was on board and he told it.

"When she was hit, the Gunner was blown out of his bunk. He climbed up on deck and started setting the depth charges on the quarterdeck to 'safe,' so they wouldn't explode if she went under.

"At first they thought she would stay afloat. They had a bunch of merchant seamen survivors they had picked up the day before. The Captain got them all out on deck, ready to abandon ship if he had to.

25

"One of the crew, an able seaman, had been operated on for appendicitis two days before. The Doc had done a good job, too. They got him up wrapped in blankets and put two lifejackets on him so's he'd have a chance. All the boats were smashed up.

"They were a sitting duck though and the U-boat fished them again. That was the finish. She started to roll under and what was left of them jumped for it. They put the appendicitis case in first but that was the last time he was seen. The Gunner was blown overboard by the second torpedo.

"When he came up the ship was going. He tried to climb aboard but it was no use. He saw her roll over until her maindeck was half under. The funnels and the gun turrets slid off into the sea. They fell right out of her. She righted then, stripped clean, and went down like the lady she was. She had given them every chance she could.

"The Old Man swam to a raft where a bunch of them were holding on and encouraged them to sing. They were covered with oil and it was hard to keep a grip. The seas were washing over them and several times during the night the raft turned over. Each time they got it righted again, but when they counted heads two or three more would have disappeared. They put the worst cases up on the raft and tried to keep their heads clear of the water. Jellyfish were biting at them and one man, who was stark naked when he got away, was so badly bitten he went crazy. Some time during the night the Captain lost his hold and slipped away. He had gone without sleep for the previous three nights and was too exhausted to hang on.

"A corvette sighted them after daylight and picked them up. They were in bad shape. Only eleven were left of the twenty-three who had started out on the raft. The Gunner said it was weeks before he felt warm again. Another officer

26

who was picked up is in the Athabaskan now," the T.G.M. concluded.

Many of the men could have told similar stories but the survivors seldom talked about their experiences, unless it was to recall some humorous incident like the time one of the officers, now on board, had been torpedoed in a corvette.

"He was in his bunk," related the Cox'n, "in pyjamas. The only man in the ship with his clothes off. He woke up when the torpedo came in and jumped for the ladder. She was going down fast. He didn't wait for a lifejacket or anything else. Seeing a raft about a hundred yards off, he dived over the side and swam to it. He must have beat the record, he was going so fast.

"He climbs aboard and looks around. 'Hello, boys,' he says, 'it's kinda cold here.' With that, he starts to button up his wet pyjamas."

The idea of buttoning up wet pyjamas in a cold North Atlantic dawn on a liferaft appealed to their sense of humour and they laughed heartily despite the grim undertone of the story. But the old hands knew their stuff. They knew the value of a good yarn in the lonely latitudes for taking men's minds off the monotony and minor discomforts that would otherwise have irked them more. Then, too, it was comforting to the new hands to realize the weight of experience behind their shipmates. They were not the kind of men who would get rattled in an emergency. The *Haida* had a really colourful crew on board.

Life aboard the ship had settled down now into what was almost a routine monotony. The ship's company had hoped to find something worth seeing at the Russian end, but the next two trips in there were similar to their first. Their anchorage was quite a distance from Murmansk and, apart from the oil tanker from which they refuelled, a few shacks

27

on shore and some Red Army sentries, there was little of interest.

Even Happy Jack, the ship's Communist, became quite unhappy about it. After a prospecting trip ashore, during which he had endeavoured to get chummy with a Red Army sentry who spoke English, he returned disappointed.

"I'm cured, sir," he informed the Engineer Officer in a burst of confidence. "If this is Communism they can have it. All I could see was just pure bloody misery. There's no brotherhood about these guys. I've wasted nine years being a Communist." With that, he took himself forward. That Red sentry will never know what a faithful follower of Communism he lost by not giving Happy Jack a drink. It's a cold climate.

The Russians, fighting for their lives, had little time for social relaxation then. All these things could come later. Meanwhile, with a German army threatening Murmansk itself, their activities were directed entirely to keeping the port open and getting more supplies South to their embattled forces.

The root of the monotony which affected the ship's company was undoubtedly the strange, uneasy quiet which had settled over the Murmansk convoy route since their arrival. This was the passage which they had anticipated would be a battle most of the way. They had come to it expectant and eager, prepared to fight bitterly, and it had hardly given them a tumble. The guns and the big armament of which they were so proud were still virgin. Not a shot had been fired in anger.

Tying up to their buoy at Scapa, when they returned there in the dusk of a winter afternoon, they listened unbelievingly to the buzzes picked up from the tanker crew which refuelled them and the hands on the different harbour craft which came alongside.

28

"Take a look around you. Look at them transports over there. They're loaded to the gunnels with troops . . . steel helmets, guns and everything. Arctic stuff, that's wot they've got. I seen it go aboard," said the Coxswain of a harbour craft as he sipped appreciatively at a cup of coffee in the messdecks.

"Sure, they're going to invade Norway. That's why the Krauts have pulled everything in. They've got it all concentrated over there, waiting for us," suggested Smoky Joe, a seaman who was as brown as an Indian.

"Aw, button it up," said the Killick. "Who the hell would want to invade Norway in December?"

"Not me," said Joe. "I don't mind taking them in but the pongos can have it from there on. I don't like mountain climbing and I didn't bring my skates."

That something was doing was quite evident to their seawise eyes from the activity in the harbour. Nevertheless, it came as a shock to them to learn that they had been ordered to half an hour's notice for steam at 0730 next morning. They had hoped they might stay there for a few days. Even Scapa looked good to them now.

"Make the most of your night in," warned the Leading Hands and the ship's company did just that. A night in harbour means a lot of nice things to seaweary men, even if there is no shore leave. One can have a bath, get one's gear fixed up and actually take one's clothes off to turn in. It had been more than a month since most of the crew had seen their bodies and they took quite an interest in bringing them to light again.

Breakfast was hardly over next morning when the pipe for special seaduty men was heard and ten minutes later hands fell in for leaving harbour. The special seaduty men had readied moorings for instant departure and at 0800, obedient to a signal received two hours previously, *Haida* slipped and proceeded to sea. Other ships had preceded her and still others, including the big grey transports, were following her out in the gloom of the winter morning.

Outside, they did not make course for Norway, despite the buzzes that were circulating wildly throughout the ship. It was North again, still further North than before, and they were above North Latitude 75, which is much further North for instance than Point Barrow in Alaska, before they found their destination. It was Spitzbergen, and the British troops they were escorting were going to garrison that bleak island wilderness in the Arctic Circle for the winter.

Still, it was a nice break, that trip. It got them away from the slow patrol duty of convoy for a few days and reminded them that *Haida* was a fast-moving destroyer when she stepped along. But when they came down to Scapa again from the lonely reaches of the Barents Sea, they found that Murmansk convoys were even more numerous than before. Every advantage was being taken of the quiet spell to rush the materials of war in ever greater measure to the now advancing Red Army.

The knowledge brought a chill of foreboding to even the most optimistic members of the ship's company. All hands realized that these convoys were too vital to the course of the war for the Krauts to permit them to pass unchallenged. Why the enemy had suddenly closed down their activities on a route which up until now they had contested so fiercely, was a question for which nobody on board seemed able to find an answer. Maybe the Nazis had something new up their sleeves. The distrust with which the crews of the Tribals looked upon the enemy was deep and profound.

CHAPTER III

Being in all respects ready for war Haida, Iroquois and Huron will slip at 0600 and proceed to sea in accordance with my 143012.

"What's the latest buzz?" queried an Asdic rating as he bummed a cigarette in the Signal office. The ship was lying at a buoy the Flow and things were quiet. The close-mouthed duty signalman there looked him over for a minute and then vouchsafed the information that something was up "down South".

"Down South," repeated the Asdic man, "What about down North? That's our interest at the moment."

"I don't know nothing about down North," muttered the signalman. "All I know is that the Victualling Assistant was ashore at the base today and he was tipped off there that we would be going South any time now."

The wardroom was equally mystified. "Stands to reason they'll try a crack at us one of these times," was the way the Engineer Officer summed up the general opinion.

The Navigator had his own ideas. "We know as much as the nigger sentry in Echo Valley," he put in, "and that's all."

"What did he know?" asked an unwary junior.

"Well, son, this nigger was on sentry duty on his first night in the valley and he thinks he hears somebody coming. 'Who dat dere?' he challenges and the echo comes back: 'Who dat dere?' "

"What did he do?"

"What would you do?" Putting his impish face within an inch of the junior's the Navigator stuck a finger in his questioner's tummy and shouted: " 'Who dat dere, say who dat dere when I say who dat dere?' And that's what we'll

31

do until we know just what the Krauts are up to," he added.

They sailed again early in December. Once more it was to the Northward and once more their convoy's destination was Murmansk. Almost immediately it was apparent that this time something was brewing. German reconnaissance planes picked them up one day out and a few more days sufficed to make them aware that U-boats were trailing astern in force, hovering on the flanks of the big convoy.

"Looks as if we might have to fight for it this time, sir," remarked the Cox'n to the Gunner T.

That able man nodded his agreement in silence. "What do you make of it Cox'n?" he asked.

"Well, sir, if they come at us with planes or subs. it's the same old stuff. We'll lose some, but they'll take a beating from us. I figure they're going to try something else. The only way they can work their subs in to do a job is to break up the convoy. If they can scatter it, they'll have a harvest all right. Maybe they've figured something."

"That's about right, Cox'n," agreed the Gunner T. "Better tip the Petty Officers and the Leading Hands to keep their men right up to scratch this trip. If we get anything it'll be their first showing and we want her to start good."

"Aye, aye, sir, I will," acknowledged the Cox'n. "The monotony's been gettin' them down a bit. What this crew needs is a touch of action."

If they had been able to look over the shoulder of the German High Admiral they would have realized that action was just what he intended to serve them, and quite a dish. Now that the North Russian escorts, with their covering planes, anti-aircraft equipment and new anti-submarine devices were making things too hot for such of the Luftwaffe or Unterseebooten as ventured to attack, he figured it was time for him to lead a trump. He could see just one way to scatter a convoy and that was to crash it with gun-power

32

the escort couldn't hope to match. The weather was all in his favour too. Visibility near zero was what he wanted.

He issued his orders and, out of a bleak Norwegian fiord a mighty German battleship slipped seaward, to be quickly enveloped in the mist of the cold, grey northern seas. To the Krauts it was their king of trumps. They knew the approximate position of the allied convoy now on its way. Under this big ship's guns they felt sure it would be forced to scatter. The U-boats hovering on the convoy's flanks would be their ace. They would be free then to come in for the kill, wreaking havoc among the scattered ships.

It was good strategy, well and carefully worked out, a nice Nazi present for Christmas. The Fuehrer would be delighted to hear how thousands of Allied sailormen met their end up in these icy seas, and at Christmas too. The name of the ship sent out to do the job was well-known. She was called the *Scharnhorst*.

Back home people were rushing to finish their Christmas shopping and wondering if Jack overseas would get his parcels of cigarettes, chocolate and other good things in time this year.

Jack himself wasn't worrying much about anything. The Tribals *Haida, Iroquois, Huron* and *Athabaskan,* in company with other destroyers, were with their convoy far up in the high latitudes. He had no illusions. Christmas would definitely be just another day at sea.

In Scapa Flow a very secret signal was received and rushed to the Commander-in-Chief. He smiled grimly as he studied it, nodding as if it confirmed what he had expected. Lifting his phone he passed a brief order. Down harbour a grey leviathan, which had been waiting quietly out in the rain-swept anchorage, slipped from her moorings and disappeared swiftly towards the North-West, accompanied by her escorting destroyers.

33

Christmas Day found the big convoy ploughing steadily through the Arctic gloom. All ships had been alerted and warned to expect attack. Aboard the merchant ships gun crews clustered beside their weapons as the vigilant escort, with all hands at Action Stations, patrolled ceaselessly on the flanks of the long lines of cargo carriers. Whatever it was, this was it. Just what to expect they did not know. The signal warning had merely alerted them to expect surface attack.

Maybe it would be destroyers or cruisers, fast raiders that would attempt to break through the protecting screen of escort ships and smash up the convoy with their guns. Maybe it would be something even bigger. Their blood tingled at the prospect of what might happen then. It would be a death or glory job, maybe both.

Next morning three British six-inch cruisers suddenly materialized to bolster up the escort forces. In one of them a Rear Admiral studied the situation which confronted him. This convoy had been under enemy surveillance for days. The Luftwaffe observers must have reported an accurate picture of its formation and escort. Some devil's plot was brewing and just what it might be was his task to probe and conjecture.

Of his surface forces, the three six-inch cruisers and the Tribal destroyers provided the main gun armament. They should be able to cope with attack by cruisers or destroyers. There was however, another possibility, and that was attack by surface battleship.

Such an attack could seriously imperil the safety of the convoy. If the formation was ever broken up and the ships scattered, the ending would be grim; the plotted dots on the chart, which represented the U-boats hovering on their flanks, were proof enough of that.

There was no margin here for error. If an enemy battle-

34

"BREAKFAST TIME BROUGHT JUGS OF COCOA."

ship struck at the convoy and found only one cruiser or a couple of destroyers in its path, the battle would be lost before it was properly joined. Any light opposition would be swept aside and the big fellow would be in among the sheep before the rest of the escort forces could get close to him. The convoy would then be scattered in a free-for-all that could have only one ending.

The cruisers, which were the main line of defence, must be concentrated therefore to meet the attack. On them the decision must be staked. The second line of defence would be the Tribal destroyers. To them the safety of the convoy would be entrusted.

Stabbing his finger at a point on the chart, the Admiral indicated where he expected the enemy to come in. It was the starboard or forward right-hand section of the long rectangle spread over miles of sea, that was the convoy.

Breakfast time brought steaming jugs of cocoa and sandwiches around to the watchful men on bridges and gun platforms aboard the escorting warships. There was a tenseness in the air now and the lookouts stared at the misty twilight which was their horizon and wondered just what might loom out of it. They didn't have to wait long.

As the murk lifted a little in belated tribute to the day and visibility increased to a mile or so, they heard the distant roll of gunfire and saw the flash of the cruisers' guns spitting back. Heeling over, they raced around the convoy towards the threatened flank, as the cruisers, looking like grey ghosts, disappeared into the wraiths of mist in the direction of the distant gunfire.

They were left alone with their thoughts then as the convoy altered course and the crackle of gunfire died away behind the shrouding curtain of mist. It was a tense period until, unexpectedly, signals came through the mist and revealed the tidings of what had transpired.

35

"It's the Scharnhorst. She pulled clear as soon as the cruisers went after her. She's broken off the engagement." The news went round the ship like wildfire.

"What's the matter with her?" asked a steward who was hauling ammunition into place. "Did she get cold feet?"

No one answered, for no one around there knew the answer to that one. But up on the bridge of the cruiser which carried his flag, the Admiral in command was making his next decision and his orders came swiftly. Cruisers were to take up station off the port quarter of the convoy now.

"Boy, this guy sure calls them," remarked Red gleefully. "Looks like he's got the Kraut's number."

The Admiral himself would probably have liked to share Red's confidence right then. He knew precisely what had happened. *Scharnhorst*, finding the concentration of fire from the cruisers blocking her path too heavy for her liking, and realizing that somehow she had not achieved the element of surprise, had withdrawn to consider the situation.

She would be back, of that he was sure, and now, with scouting destroyers probing through the grey horizons about the convoy, and alert radar operators checking for the slightest sign of movement anywhere beyond, he had concentrated his cruisers at the point where he believed the next attack would develop.

Somewhere to the southward he was aware that a battleship of the K.G.V. class was on its way to support him but she was still too far off to arrive in time to give him any assistance in this phase of the action. If she was lucky she might intercept the *Scharnhorst* on her way back, not much of a hope really in the case of a ship of the *Scharnhorst's* speed in these gloom-enshrouded waters.

"She's coming in, sir, right on this bearing," reported an officer, and he had hardly spoken when they heard the crack

36

of her guns and two great columns of water spouted to starboard between them and the next cruiser. They forged ahead to close immediately, trying for a range that would make their smaller guns effective.

Once again the speeding Tribals swept around the convoy as they shepherded the merchant ships away from the fight and once again the Admiral's judgment had been correct. He had placed his three cruisers directly in the *Scharnhorst's* path. Once more the roll of gunfire sounded briskly at first and then died away as the convoy and its escort put distance between themselves and the battle.

This time the engagement was not broken off and the Tribal crews had to content themselves with the scanty news from whatever signals they could pick up. From these they gathered that the cruisers had closed the range sufficiently to make their lighter armament effective and were hitting the *Scharnhorst,* although they were taking punishment from the big guns of the enemy vessel too.

The *Scharnhorst* however was making off to the South-East. Probably she had been warned of the approach of the British battleship and, finding the cruisers again blocking her attempt to reach the convoy, was making back to her hideout before she could be intercepted.

But this time, the cruisers stayed with her, clinging like leeches and dodging grimly as she turned her great armament on them in an effort to shake them off. If they could hold on to her and signal her position, there was still a chance she might be intercepted.

Aboard the K.G.V. class battleship, H.M.S. Duke of York, engineers and stokers worked like Trojans to get every ounce of steam that could be raised. Slowly but inexorably the plot of her position moved across the chart, closer and closer to the point where her course would intercept that of the fleeing Nazi battleship.

37

Like hounds unleashed, the *Duke of York's* escorting destroyers were sent ahead of her now to range through the darkness of the Arctic gloom and locate the enemy. Guided by the signals sent by the British cruisers hanging persistently to the *Scharnhorst's* heels, they came upon her.

The destroyers had a definite objective, a job which they must do. Somehow or other the big German battlewagon must be slowed down so that the speeding British battleship astern of them could close the range and bring her big guns to bear on the enemy. This was an operation which destroyers were designed and equipped to do and they went to it with a will.

Braving the curtain of gunfire from *Scharnhorst's* armament, they slashed at her through the darkness with their torpedoes. Many missed, for *Scharnhorst* was taking every possible evasive action, twisting and weaving to make herself a difficult target. Then came a particularly daring attack as a destroyer raced in to a range almost incredibly close in view of the size and power of the target, and let go at her with four torpedoes.

One struck home. As the destroyer heeled over and turned away, observers on her bridge saw the telltale flash of the explosive down towards the big ship's after end. A little later the hit was unofficially confirmed by *Scharnhorst* herself when she was found to have suddenly slowed down.

Their objective accomplished, the daring destroyers, some of them heavily punished by *Scharnhorst's* guns, sheered off now to clear the range for the *Duke of York*. The big British battleship had closed the gap and from far in the distant gloom came the thunder of her main armament as she opened fire.

Great shell splashes erupted in the sea around the doomed Nazi as the tremendous projectiles from the *Duke of York's* fifteen-inch guns fell in her vicinity. More salvos thundered out as range corrections were made and then came a hit which sent flames leaping up the Nazi's superstructure.

She was stopped dead in her tracks in the sea and into her burning hull crashed shell after shell until all her return fire was smothered and she lay, a blazing, devastated hulk, on the surface of the water. From the *Duke of York* the call came then for those destroyers with torpedoes left to close in and give the big German the coup-de-grace.

That was the end of the *Scharnhorst*. Through the darkness, smoke and haze, observers watched as the blurred glimmer of flame in the Arctic night that was the doomed enemy flickered and died and she slipped under the cold, leaden seas. It was over then. That particular threat to the Murmansk convoys had been dealt with and only a handful of dazed and shivering survivors were left to mark her passing.

The news came to the Tribals as they brought their convoy through the approaches to Russia. It was a brief message which stated simply that *Scharnhorst* had been sunk. All hands cheered the victory. They were surprised at the speed with which the pattern of events had been woven after the action was joined, a handful of hours covering the action from beginning to end. It was very tantalizing, moreover, to have a major sea action take place almost under their noses and not have the opportunity to fire a gun. They felt they had missed out on that one, and not even their bringing the convoy safely to harbour could make up for it.

However, they could have their belated Christmas dinner now and that was something. All the makings had been put on board before they left Scapa and the cooks had many willing helpers as they set about preparing it.

"Boy, I bet this old turkey came right from Ontario,"

said Red as he looked admiringly over a plump bird brought up from storage.

"That's a Chinese turkey," the Leading Cook informed him.

"How can you tell?" asked Red, too cheerful to be suspicious.

"Easy, you just look in the bag for the good earth. If it's in the bag, you've got it."

"Is that so?" said Red, remembering, with an effort, that it pays to be polite to the gentlemen who wield the skillet. "I dunno anything about where it came from, but one thing I do know, and that's where it's going."

"Attaboy Red," encouraged the helpers.

"Thanks, gentlemen," said Red as he held the bird up and was about to oblige with further details when the ringing of the buzzers sounding anti-aircraft Action Stations sent all hands running to their posts.

The fighting ships had left the convoy and anchored in lonely Vaenga Bay. It was a quiet harbour surrounded by desolate, snow-covered hills, but the Luftwaffe, seeking revenge for the loss of the *Scharnhorst* had decided to attempt to even up the one-sided score.

Swooping in low over the hills and zooming upwards as they crossed the Bay, the German planes came in to attack. If they had hoped to find the ships napping, they were bitterly disappointed. Anti-aircraft guns, both ashore and afloat, roared angrily into action, throwing up such a barrage of steel that the planes circled ineffectually, dropped a few distant bombs and retired precipitately.

That little matter over, the Tribal crews continued their dinner preparations. Christmas being over, most of the usual ceremonies were omitted, but they decorated the messdecks to the best of their ability and Santa Claus dis-

40

"THEY SANG EVERY SONG THEY COULD REMEMBER."

tributed a Christmas stocking to each man after they had eaten to repletion.

The Christmas stockings were ditty-bags, packed by thoughtful hands in the homes in far-off Canada. They gave the men much pleasure, and also amusement, as each man had to open his ditty-bag and show the contents to the others. In one of them, for a lark, someone had inserted a very "Hollywoody" tie. This was immediately put round the Cox'n's neck and tied in a big bow.

They had a get-together afterwards, all hands assembling in the messdecks for a sing-song. They sang every song they could remember, falling back on old favourites like *Sweet Adeline* as the evening advanced. The final number was the lusty, ribald and largely unprintable song of the Tribals.

New hands stared agape as that number was rendered by an officer who had been three times torpedoed, and he sang it in a sweet, clear voice that completely belied the libellous words.

The tune was *Bless 'Em All* and the first verse was:

> *A Tribal was leaving the Flow*
> *Bound for Spitzbergen's shores,*
> *With two leaky tanks and the pumps on the bum*
> *And empty shells in the stores;*
> *Said a tired old plumber who was just signing off*
> *To another poor sap signing on;*
> *"You'll get no Secure in this two-funnelled sewer,*
> *So cheer up my lads, bless 'em all."*

Into the chorus came the swelling voices of the ship's company, with a roar that rose to the watching signalmen up on the dark bridge:

> *"Bless 'em all, bless 'em all,*
> *The Captain, the Jimmy and all,*

41

Bless all the seamen and gunners' mates, too,
Bless all the stokers and their dirty crew,
For we're saying goodbye to them all
As over the billows we sail.
You'll get no Secure in this two-funnelled sewer
So cheer up, my lads, bless 'em all."

Next morning, *Haida* and her sisters sailed out from the cold, encircling snow-covered hills of Russia on passage back to Scapa Flow. Their part in the *Scharnhorst* action had been a minor one but they had sniffed the scent of battle and thirsted for more. There was a feeling in the wind that now the *Scharnhorst* was gone, something else might be brewing. Events were casting their long shadows before.

CHAPTER IV

Being in all respects ready for war slip at 0800 and proceed in accordance with my 2211430 to join Force 26 under C. in C. Plymouth.

"Eddystone Lighthouse in sight bearing O seven two," called the Officer of the Watch down the voicepipe.

The Navigator, in his domain directly beneath the bridge known as the "Plot", to which the voicepipe led, acknowledged the information and turned to glance at the chart. This was the room in which the ship's position and course was plotted and the chart of this particular area was spread out on a long table across one end of the cabin. On it was the course the ship must take to enter Plymouth Harbour.

Racks of other charts filled the space beneath the long table and above it was a gyro compass card, on which was repeated the ship's course. Another glass-topped plotting table and other gear filled up the space on one side of the room. Along the other side was a cushioned locker seat on which the Navigator often slept at sea.

Satisfied that the course was correct he returned to the bell-mouthed end of the bridge voicepipe beside him and called up, "Plot-Bridge!"

"Bridge-Plot," came the instant acknowledgment.

"O.K." called up the Navigator, "alter course at eight o'clock to O four five. I'll give you the next alteration in a few minutes."

"O four five at eight o'clock," repeated the Officer of the Watch.

An old landmark to some of the crew, the Eddystone Light was new to many and they looked with interest at

43

the slender column built on the low rock reef which had brought disaster to so many ships until the light was built. Near it was the base of a former lighthouse which the sea had overwhelmed. Down South here the sun was shining brightly, although it was January, and visibility was perfect. Inshore, clear in the winter sunshine they could see the green hills of Devon.

This weather presented an amazing contrast with the dark gloom of the Northern seas. It was like coming back into the daylight and the world of reality after a long sojourn in darkness. They looked upon it with the air of men who are thankful but not quite sure whether they dare accept it yet as the truth. In their minds they still belonged too much to the dark and lonely seas down North.

"You guys better be on your toes around here," remarked a stoker who had stepped up on deck for a breath of air to one of the torpedomen standing by the tubes.

"Is that so?" returned the torpedoman impolitely.

"It's just seventy miles over there to the French coast," continued the stoker, "and this is a hot spot. Them E boats comes over here every night and sometimes their destroyers too."

"What about their planes?" asked a seaman gunner.

The group fell silent at that. Seventy miles is a matter of less than fifteen minutes for fighter planes. There would be bombers also.

"Just what I was telling this guy," continued the stoker. "You blokes better be on your toes around here. If you let us get sunk you better go with her, or you'll wish you had the next time you meet up with us."

"Aw boil your oil," retorted the seaman, "if we get sunk it'll be because you guys can't keep that sewing machine of yours going."

His face, like those of his mates, was thoughtful however

44

as he left the grinning stoker and walked forward. This English Channel had a hot name all right. There had been lots of gloomy buzzes when they left Scapa. "It's E-boat alley for you blokes," had been the supply boat's farewell, "no sea-room at all and you'll probably get sunk in the first month."

Shrilly along the decks came the whistle of the Bosun's pipe: "Secure defence stations. Hands fall in for entering harbour. All men not in the rig of the day off the upper deck."

In the shelter of a headland which extended seaward on the port hand the ship was approaching the seagate. This was the usual narrow passage between two small ships, known as gate-ships, to which the boom defence nets, made of thick steel cables suspended from floating steel buoys are attached at their seaward end. Between the ships is a short, similar boom net which can be opened to allow passage and closed behind each ship or group of ships passing through. The nets extended from the beach on one side to a great breakwater which jutted out on the starboard side and closed off the open end of the horseshoe-shaped outer harbour.

Permission to enter was requested of the guardian forts covering the entrance. This was received and the ship slowed to pass through the gate. As she came in a voice hailed them through a loudspeaker on the starboard gate ship.

"Have you any casualties or survivors?"

Loud and clear the hail, made to each entering ship, brought home to the listening crew of the Tribal the fact that this was indeed the Front Line. Out behind them, across the narrow channel seas lay the enemy-held coastline of Europe, with its fortified defences, its harbours, planes and fighting craft. In the past three years there must have come in here from the no-man's land that lay between the

45

two coasts many ships which had answered the hail at this seagate in the affirmative.

As *Haida* steamed up the harbour they saw the high front of Plymouth Hoe, with its terraced esplanade, swimming pools, bandstands and memorials which overlooked the entrance rising directly ahead. Channels led off to inner harbours on either hand. *Haida* swung left, to port, past a low island with ancient, battlemented walls.

"Drake's Island," commented the Navigator; "that's where the old boy went when he wanted to get away from his wife."

Between old stone docks, battlements and a scenic roadway on one hand, and green wooded hills on the other, the winding waterway went up until it opened into a long, busy harbour.

"There she is," pointed out a gunner, "Devonport Dockyard itself."

The pipe for "Still" sounded along the decks and every man stiffened to attention. Another destroyer was passing, one of the famous Hunt Class. Her crew, at attention, were looking up at the big Tribal. The pipe shrilled again, twice, and the order came to stand at ease.

"Juicer," commented a seaman, "they're sure pusser here." (The term "pusser" pertains to all things of the Navy, from clothes to anchors, as distinguished from things bought or made on "civvy street").

Past an old four-stacker which had reached her last anchorage the ship steamed on. To starboard, on the right hand, was the dockyard. It was a tremendous place, stretching for several miles along the waterfront, and overflowing here and there across the harbour.

Ships of all types lay at anchored buoys in the stream and alongside the docks. Here the great cranes of building stocks towered above a ship under construction, and in the maze of workshops, tidal basins and drydocks could be seen battleships, cruisers, submarines, destroyers, frigates, corvettes and many other craft.

"Wires and fenders to starboard side. Ship will secure alongside," came the order, and the waiting seamen, scenting shore leave, worked with a will. Fenders were hauled into position to cushion the hull from the dock; wires hauled round and led through the eyes and heaving lines coiled ready for use.

That done, they straightened up to watch the Captain take her in. They were unusually proud of the way he handled her. A destroyer can be quite a handful to bring alongside, but there was no hesitancy or creeping in and never a bump. It was done in a swift, competent manner that never failed to bring a look of surprised admiration to the faces of the waiting dockers, which was a tribute of some gratification to the crew. This, they felt, was the way a destroyer should come in.

Messengers, mail and visitors were waiting alongside to come aboard and the ship was soon buzzing with news. According to the visitors *Haida* was to be based here from now on. Something big was coming and the Tribals had been brought down to strengthen the Channel forces. Best of all, to the ship's company, was the buzz that boiler cleaning, repairs and the installation of new radar equipment would keep them alongside for several days. That would mean shore leave for both watches. Four months of Arctic seas had left money in their pockets. Now they could spend some.

While they worked as they awaited the official pronouncement they learned what they could of their new job. It was a hot area, they were told. By day the Channel seas, except for coastal movements, were deserted. By night it was a different story.

Slipping out as darkness fell, Motor Torpedo Boats and

Motor Gun Boats, small, fast, powerfully-armed craft which could operate close inshore in shallow water, minelayers, patrol craft and destroyers would make for the middle reaches and the enemy coast, seeking Nazi patrols or unwary enemy convoys. From the German-held ports on the French side would come enemy E boats, the Nazi counterpart of the M.T.B.'s and M.G.B.'s and other craft on like missions off the English shores.

Starshell would flare in that world of darkness and lines of tracer arch across the night sky as the opposing forces encountered each other and fought it out in short but fierce and spirited engagements. When the dawn broke over the troubled waters they would be gone, leaving only the mute evidence of some drifting wreckage, a handful of survivors or a crippled craft limping home while its tense crew watched the skies.

"What's this starshell stuff they talk about?" asked a new Communications Rating as he lugged a shellcase across the deck and passed it down to another hand in a barge alongside. The ship was de-ammunitioning, sending all her ammunition ashore according to the usual precaution exercised whenever repairs involving a stay of several days were to be made.

The men had paused for a moment, waiting for more stuff to come up from below; the job was nearly finished.

"Don't ask me, I'm an Oerlikon gunner," replied the man beside him. "Ask the Gunner's Mate. There he is now."

"Ask me what?" queried the Gunner's Mate, overhearing the last few words.

"This guy's never seen a starshell. He wants to know sumpin about it."

"He's seen plenty. He's been carrying it all morning. I should think he's seen enough by now. At least I have

48

if he hasn't. What's your trouble with starshell, lad? Don't you know one when you see it?"

"No, this is my first ship."

"Well, you've come to the right place for you'll see plenty here. Any of you other guys want to know about starshell?"

"Sure," answered half a dozen men in the vicinity.

"That's good. Never hesitate to ask questions about anything you don't understand for any one of you is liable to be called on for any kind of a job here if we have casualties.

"Now I could be technical but you wouldn't understand me, not all of you anyway, so I'll stick to plain language. Here's a four-point-seven starshell right here. It looks much the same as an ordinary shell in shape although it's marked different. Now, in the nose of this shell there is a fuse, and this fuse can be set to explode at the required height and distance. To set the fuse you simply turn this marked ring here. All your ranges are right on it.

"Say you want to illuminate a suspected target at 7,000 yards. O.K. You turn the ring until the mark is at 7,000, then you fire the shell. It comes out of the gun like any other shell, carries on until it reaches the required height and distance and then it bursts.

"Now, you want to know what happens then . . . how it lights up the target. Well, this is what happens. The inside of this shell is not filled with the usual high explosive like other types of shell. Inside this shell is a flare and a small parachute. The small charge which causes the burst ejects the parachute and the flare, which hangs below it in a canister suspended by steel wires. The flare gives out its light as the parachute drops it slowly towards the surface so that full advantage can be taken of the thirty seconds or so during which it is illuminating the sea beneath it as it comes down. The parachute itself is braced with wires like an umbrella. These are folded down when the parachute is

49

inside the shell but the moment it is released they spring open, so that the parachute, which looks like a big handkerchief, spreads out and takes the weight of the canister containing the flare.

"Usually more than one starshell is fired at a time to illuminate and silhouette a suspected enemy. The bloke who sees the other guy first has the best chance, for he can range his guns and observe the fall of his shot on the enemy in the light of the starshell he has fired. I remember one night in my last ship we picked up a surfaced U-boat in the North Atlantic. It was as black as the ace of spades that night. He was two miles away, but the starshell showed him up as plain as day and we got him with our guns."

"How about searchlights . . . don't they use them?" asked the Communications Hand.

"Sure, but you don't do it often if you want to stay alive, son. A searchlight gives your own position away immediately and will be no good to you against an enemy at a distance. The starshell shows him up without illuminating you. You're like the guy in the dark shooting at a bloke in the light. You can see him but he can't see you. The enemy, of course, also use starshell. Theirs has a kind of greenish glow to it. Searchlights are useful for close work at times but they're a dead giveaway. Well, here's the rest of the stuff from below. Everybody happy? . . . O.K., let's finish it."

Later, when the Secure had been piped and the hands were below at noon dinner, they heard the quartermaster piping the announcement of first and second leaves, and learned that first leave travelling warrants would be available in the ship's office at two o'clock.

There was quick and excited discussion in the messdecks then, all hands smiling cheerfully. Leave was to be granted to the entire ship's company in two watches. Half would go

50

"I'M NOT SAYING SHE'LL GO FOR YOU."

on first leave and the other half on second leave when the first returned.

"How about it, Scotty . . . is it Glassgy this time?" a big slow-spoken gunner of Scottish extraction was asked.

"Aye, it'll be the big smoke first, then Glesca," he answered happily. "Ah've an uncle there ah've never seen."

"You an' the Bluenoses! How many of you are going this time?"

"What's the matter with Glasgow?" asked the Bluenose Leading Hand from Halifax.

That was the signal for an immediate heartfelt rendition of *I Belong to Glasgow,* with mouth organ accompaniment.

There was much discussion about where to go. Many had relatives or friends in different parts of the Island Kingdom whom they intended to visit, and sailors on leave have a capacity for covering distances that is a never ending source of wonder. Sixty hours for each watch, the first leave in six months, is brief by any other than naval standards, which recognize only the exigencies of the service. However, in that time the men went far afield.

Lined up and inspected before departure they were a well-washed, clean-shaven, good-looking bunch of Jack Tars. They marched out from the ship along roadways heavy with traffic and up the long ramp to a high, stone-arched gate in the guarded walls of the dockyard. Royal Marine Police sentries checked them over at this point and passed them out to the Albert Road and the freedom of Britain.

Most of the leave men caught a bus for the station, but a Petty Officer and three hands decided to go up to Plymouth, of which Devonport is really a suburb, and pay a few calls there first before catching the night train out.

The appearance of "the worst-blitzed city in Britain" gave them quite a shock. The city was an empty shell of roofless churches, ruined buildings and blasted homes. The main business centre was simply a flat heap of raked rubble. The streets through it, with their big waterpipes along the side of the road for fighting air-raid fires, had been cleared, but one could look across from block to block over the rubble of what had been stores and shops of all descriptions before the bombers came. On little white markers, like a graveyard, were the names of the stores that once had stood there.

As they stood there and looked at it one of them recognized a passing R.N. Petty Officer and called him over.

"Quite a mess," they remarked after the introductions had been made, nodding at the rubble.

"Yes, I was taking my course here when most of it happened. They came over day and night for twenty-nine days," he told them.

"Holy smoke, did you make it?"

"It wasn't too bad at Devonport. Bad enough, but not as bad as it was up here. We studied in the daytime and every time the alarm went we either dived for the shelter or lent a hand to the anti-aircraft gun crews. At night we turned out to fight fires and pull out the wounded and the bodies. The civil authorities couldn't keep up with it. A lot of their men were away and a lot more were knocked out.

"I didn't expect to pass when I went up for the course, and then, when we didn't get any time to do much studying, I felt sure I'd fail. However, much to our surprise, they passed the whole class. Either the instructors were too fagged out to face us again or they figured we had earned it. Come and have a beer. There's a pub just round the corner in what's left of that hotel over there."

Sixty hours soon pass and when the first leavers returned there was a general exchange of names and phone numbers with the easy familiarity of the sea.

"I'm not saying she'll go for you," one Jack was overheard telling his opposite number. "She treated me all right. She's got a flat and she lives there with her mother. The old lady's a bit deaf but she's a good sport. I told the Babe about you being my chum and gave you a good build-up so it's worth a show. That cocky Oerlikon gunner tried to horn in the second night when he met us in a pub but she shut him off fast. He had it!"

By the end of the week the leave period was ended and all hands were on board again. Amongst them they brought back quite a bit of news. Two new Fleet Class destroyers, the *Algonquin* and the *Sioux*, had been commissioned for the Royal Canadian Navy and were expected to come south to the Channel. Those who had been in London, "the big smoke", reported nightly bombing, but it had not cramped their style.

There were big buzzes from the shipyards up North. Strange-looking secret ships were being built there that looked very different to the other battleships and aircraft carriers on the stocks. They were very hush-hush and it was rumoured they were to be used for the invasion of Europe.

The boys on leave had been impressed with the tremendous numbers of landing craft they had spotted under construction. Every little boatyard on every little waterway seemed to be building them, and the convoys were bringing over additional hundreds every trip. Something big must be coming up soon, was the general reaction to that news.

Something was already up for the Tribals, as they soon discovered, something that meant exercise after exercise, by day and by night in the Channel seas.

Haida, Athabaskan and *Iroquois* had been joined by a British Tribal, H.M.S. Ashanti. This force now became the initial establishment of the 10th Destroyer Flotilla, a name that was destined to make history. *Iroquois*, after her long

53

tour of operational duty down North (she had been commissioned since January 1943, more than a year previously) required a refit. She was relieved therefore by *Huron*, which came down from Scapa after another Murmansk trip. *Iroquois* was then ordered to proceed to Halifax, Nova Scotia, and have a long refit carried out there. Another British Tribal Destroyer, H.M.S. Tartar, now joined them as Flotilla Leader under Captain D. To this new 10th Destroyer Flotilla was given a dual task, a related duty that called for both offensive and defensive operations.

As preparations went steadily forward for the projected invasion of France, more and more amphibious exercises were taking place along the English Channel coast to ready the growing fleets of invasion craft for the big event. These required adequate protection to seaward to prevent enemy raiders from slipping through and mauling the lightly-armed landing craft.

Protection to seaward also was required for the big convoys now being brought directly into Channel ports from North America and other areas. These, loaded with invasion supplies which the already overburdened roads and railways could not hope to cope with, offered particularly tempting targets to enemy surface raiding forces and U-boats based on the adjacent French coast.

The offensive part of their operations was to seek out and destroy enemy surface fighting ships based on French Channel ports and in the Bay of Biscay. In these areas Allied intelligence had spotted at least twenty destroyers, including some of the big, heavily gunned Narvik class, as well as Roeders, which was the name given to the improved Narvik class. These were even bigger and armed with guns of greater calibre than the Tribals.

A brisk sea fight in the Bay of Biscay, which occurred the day after the *Scharnhorst* action, had seen the British cruisers

Glasgow and *Enterprise,* the latter under the command of a Captain of the Royal Canadian Navy, destroy one Narvik and two Elbing class destroyers out of a large enemy destroyer force which they had sighted and pursued. This action, however, good as it was, did not suffice to secure the position. The enemy still had sufficient forces to offer a serious threat to Channel operations.

Force 26, which the R.C.N. Tribals had originally been assigned to, was maintained as a tactical unit. The two light cruisers H.M.S. Bellona and H.M.S. Black Prince had been added to the Plymouth Command. When destroyers of the 10th D.F. operated with the cruisers the combined unit was known as Force 26. As a striking force for offensive operations it was a well-conceived combination, providing a force capable of dealing effectively with enemy surface fighting ships which might be encountered in their own waters.

There were, of course, many other ships in the Western Approaches Command. The small but highly effective Hunt Class destroyers were used extensively, as were the escort destroyers, M.T.B.'s, M.G.B.'s, frigates, trawlers, minesweepers and other craft. The cruisers and the 10th D.F. were however the "big punch", used primarily for the offensive operations of the guardian forces of the Western Approaches.

To be efficient as a night-fighting unit, practically all surface Channel operations taking place under cover of darkness, extensive exercises were embarked upon with vigour now. The Communications Rating who had been so anxious to find out about starshell stared in amazement, as did many of his mates, as they finally saw it used in operations.

Dividing their forces into two units, the cruisers and the ships of the 10th D.F. practised night encounters, competing to see who would be the first to locate and identify the other. It was a proud moment for the Force which could fire its starshell first and see the ships of the other side silhouetted several miles in the distance and looking like miniatures in the spreading light of the starshells.

Nightfighting is an art in itself and the crews had much to learn. Maintaining station had a number one priority, for a good maxim in nightfighting is that "those who are not with us are against us." Ships keeping station as a compact unit can smash into an enemy force, disperse it and destroy it much more efficiently and with a great deal less hazard to themselves than if they scatter. It is easy to fire on one's friends in the dark, especially if they come up from unexpected quarters.

In the daytime, torpedo shoots, towing evolutions so that a damaged ship could be taken quickly in tow and hauled clear — gunnery exercises and anti-aircraft practice combined to bring the ship's company to a high state of efficiency.

An Air Force pilot towing a sleeve target, a cylindrical canvas affair shaped like a big sausage open at both ends, well astern of his plane thought they were a little too efficient one afternoon.

The anti-aircraft gunners on the Oerlikons and multiple-barreled pom-pom fired a few bursts a little ahead of the target this day and a little too close to the plane to suit the nervous pilot's disposition. He quickly signalled "I'm pulling this target, not pushing it!"

It was a pleasant period even if a busy one. Interspersed with the exercises were night Channel patrols for convoy protection and actual raiding trips sweeping along within a handful of miles off the French coast to give them experience.

The weather was a gift from heaven. Day after day the sun shone warmly from cloudless skies and all hands revelled

56

in it. Afternoons in harbour found many of the ship's company stripped to the waist and stretched out in the health-giving rays. To them this was really living, after the long months of cold and darkness in the Arctic. To find weather like this, in February and March, was an event and a remarkably delightful event at that. Their eyes and faces showed its tonic effect.

Night leave ashore was fairly frequent and the ship's company were making friends. Plymouth's pubs, of which quite a few were still in operation, even if they had retreated in some cases to the basement, found plenty of customers for their innocuous wartime beer. The seamen liked the friendly atmosphere and the civilians here could not do enough for them. Sharing the common peril of a frontline port, they knew only too well the toll that was taken regularly of the lads who went out to do the fighting that was the only guarantee of their continued safety.

Then, too, the raiding expeditions off the French coast carried out by Force 26 gave a zest to life that was exhilarating after the watchful monotony of the lonely Arctic seas.

It gave them quite a thrill to slip from their mooring buoy and sail down harbour as the sun slanted earthwards towards the horizon and the long shadows of evening came. Shoreward they could see the people moving around, many of them stopping to wave to them. For the seamen this was always goodbye. Each time they sailed they looked long and hard at the things of the land, conscious always that it might be for the last time.

With the freshness of the evening breeze ruffling their hair as they passed through the seagate to the darkening waters of the open Channel, they set their course for the enemy-held shores of France, sailing the seas that Drake, Nelson, Cochrane and Frobisher had known, and wondering sometimes what the ghosts of these great Admirals would

57

think if they could look down upon them now. Times had changed. The possession of a single Tribal destroyer then could have dictated the history of the world.

It was good, too, returning in the morning, home from their foray when the housewives were scrubbing down their front steps and crews who had been in harbour all night were still rubbing the sleep from their eyes. These first operations uncovered no targets in February and March but they were productive of incidents which indicated the tense watchfulness in these waters.

Their journeys were not always uneventful. One night one of the cruisers, operating with the Tribals some seven miles off the French coast, made a contact which at first seemed to be a ship. The Force snapped into action right away and raced to close.

Starshell shot up followed by high explosive shells and a burst of flame appeared where the shells had landed. It looked for a moment like a hit. It was, too, only on a hay-stack or farmhouse on one of several small islands just off the French coast.

Every one of the enemy's invasion-conscious garrisons, from Norway to the Spanish border must have been alerted that night, wondering if this was the beginning. Perhaps even the mighty Rommel may have been called from his uneasy slumbers.

On another occasion, during a mid-channel patrol, *Haida, Athabaskan* and *Huron* felt sure they had flushed an E boat at last. It appeared to be crossing ahead of them at slow speed.

Increasing revolutions, they took up attack formation and raced up for a kill. Speeding ahead and slightly to port *Athabaskan* switched on her searchlights as she came abeam of the target so that *Haida,* racing up in the darkness astern

58

could crush through it with her knifelike bows and send it to the bottom.

Peering intently into the darkness *Haida's* bridge crew saw *Athabaskan's* searchlight switch on, and there directly in their path was the target.

"Port Fifteen" came the crisp order and *Haida* swung to avoid ramming as *Athabaskan's* searchlight switched off and one of her own switched on. There, just clearing their direct path as the destroyer swung to port, was a motor fishing boat, her crew standing on deck with gaping mouths looking up at the sinister spectacle of sudden death which had materialized so suddenly out of the darkness.

"These unmentionable fishermen," commented an annoyed Midshipman, "they take an awful chance when they disregard orders and come outside their area."

He was right. Fishing craft operating outside their prescribed areas in these waters were highly suspect. The enemy shore was too close to allow chances to be taken; enemy agents would have given much to cross that narrow strip. E boats passed through here frequently at night, too. If a fisherman, actuated by a desire to get more fish, went five miles further to seaward than he should be, he took quite a chance. It was unlikely that this particular craft would stray again. Death had brushed him too closely, and when he reached shore he would have some exceedingly awkward questions to answer.

By now the night operations off the French coast had familiarized the crews with the coastwise navigation lights there and the habits of the enemy. Sweeping in, gun crews at Action Stations, they often sighted the lighthouses at Ile de Bas, Ile de Vierge and other points as they made their traverse.

Some nights, when the enemy had spotted them, all the coastal lights would be turned out. Sometimes the Tribal's bridge crews would note them being switched off as they closed in. It was strange warfare, speeding along under the stars, looking inshore at the dark, looming bulk of the land. Often they wondered how the people were making out there, how long it would be before the day of liberation came to lift the darkness which now hung over the land of France. Being impatient, they even had the audacity to wonder if the Germans ever moved any ships on this coast at all; if, despite the heavy bombing, they were still using rail transport to Brest and the West.

Nights were coming soon, however, when this steady, persistent vigilance was going to show results that effectively stopped all grumbles on that score.

"PEERING INTENTLY INTO THE DARKNESS."

CHAPTER V

Being in all respects ready for war Force 26 will carry out
Operation Tunnel in accordance with orders. Destroyers
Haida, Athabaskan, Huron, Ashanti will slip at 2100 and
proceed in company with H.M.S. Black Prince.

A "Naafi" launch (Navy, Army, Air Force Institute to the
uninitiated) its foredeck loaded with sides of beef and pork,
the pork being most predominant, besides sacks of potatoes
and cartons of packaged and tinned victuals, came chugging
across the harbour in the early afternoon sunlight and
approached a Tribal class destroyer lying at a buoy in the
stream.

Sticking his head out of the little wheelhouse, into which
he must have squeezed his bulk with difficulty, the rotund
operator, a cheerful-looking bloke in cloth cap and nondescript jacket and pants, eased the coloured muffler around
his throat and hailed the ship. The hoarse interrogation
sounded like "Hayday?"

Answered in the affirmative by the quartermaster, he
steered his unwieldly craft alongside, cut the engine, squeezed
successfully through the narrow doorway out onto the deck
and tossed up the forward mooring line. Down aft another
figure, recumbent until now in a coil of rope, came to life
and threw up the after line.

A working party of seamen, lounging by the torpedo tubes
awaiting the arrival of the launch, took the lines and made
them fast. That done, a Petty Officer, commonly known as a
P.O., accompanied by two of the ratings from the working
party, jumped down onto the foredeck of the launch and
proceeded to check the stores. As each item was checked
it was passed up to the waiting hands on deck, to the accom-

paniment of a free flow of unvarnished criticism and comment.

"More pork Joe? Whadda ya do with all the meat? So help me I'm going to turn Yid after this war and eat nuthin but Kosher grub. If only Alberta could see me now," commented a Westerner.

"She'd murder you," remarked Red unfeelingly.

"Don't you guys from Toronto ever go to school? Don't they never teach you there's other parts of this country outside the Toronto city limits?" asked the Westerner, looking serious.

"Oh sure," returned Red politely. "There's Hamilton and the prairies. That's where we get the beef and the wheat from. After that it's just bush and a bunch of Indians."

"Put it down! Put it down!" warned the P.O. as the Westerner lugged up a leg of beef and looked speculatively at the grinning Red. Reluctantly he hefted it to his shoulder, shook his head sadly and carried it forward.

"I wonder where all the steaks do go?" asked a young O.D. (Ordinary Seaman) in a plaintive tone.

A Killick, his rating marked by the wearing of an anchor on his sleeve, looked the O.D. over slowly.

"You're wondering. Don't you know where they go son?"

"Well where do they go?" muttered the O.D. apprehensively.

"I'll tell you where they go son," the Killick informed him. "They go to the guys that are fighting this war. That's the Air Force, the birdie boys. If you stick around long enough you'll find out that the Air Force get everything, and I mean everything. Now get cracking an' shift that pig. It ain't goin' to walk to the galley by itself."

Around the guns the crews, stripped to the waist, were

62

busy oiling, setting and adjusting their charges. Up in bosun's chairs, high on the forward funnel, two seamen engaged in scraping paint blisters stopped work to holler down to a passing shipmate.

"What's the buzz, cuzz . . . any shore leave?" queried the lowest one hopefully.

"Shore leave?" repeated he who was asked in tones of amazement. "What's that? A cruiser drill? I only been on this packet six months."

"Aw, don't you know nuthin'?"

"Not a thing brother. I ain't got no crystal ball. Somebody said the Jimmy (First Lieutenant) told the Cox'n to pipe Secure in ten minutes so as we could turn in. But somebody's always saying sumpin' an' I ain't no crystal ball. Besides I'm married. I'm not interested in shore leave. I'm not like you guys. Why should I be?"

Ignoring a request "to come up here an' learn sumpin'", the loquacious one went on his way.

Down aft on the quarterdeck came a movement which presaged something. The Officer of the Day became suddenly conspicuous. The seaboat slipped from her mooring astern and came alongside the quarterdeck jumping ladder. The Captain appeared and climbed down into the boat. Casting off, it went upharbour to the next buoy where the *Athabaskan* was lying. Her Commanding Officer climbed down into the boat. From there it proceeded into Flagstaff Steps. The Commanding Officer of *Huron* was waiting for them with a staff car. Climbing in, the three C.O.'s drove off.

"They're going to a conference at A.C.H.Q." (Area Combined Headquarters), remarked a watching signalman to his mate on the bridge. "Wonder if we're going out tonight?" As he spoke the Secure sounded along the decks and all hands except the duty watch knocked off.

63

A few went below to seek relaxation in sleep but, for the most part, the hands off duty found sheltered spots in the sun, up on the gundecks or around the tubes. There they relaxed according to their tastes. Some read, some slept and some sunbathed. Others sat around indulging in desultory conversation, or "fanning the breeze" as the lowerdeck vernacular describes it best.

"Bunker", the newest recruit on board, a nondescript mongrel with a strong seasoning of Airedale in his composition, was standing with his head cocked to one side watching a leather glove being dangled in a gunner's hand. The guncrew had brought him on board on their return from leave, securing the Officer of the Day's permission for a "purebred Airedale pup".

"We paid cash for it sir. Here's the receipt," said Red eagerly the night they had arrived with it. "The man said it had a real pedigree too. He couldn't find the papers handy but he's going to send them on."

"How much did you pay for it?" asked the Officer.

"Seven and sixpence, sir. It was all we had left between us," Red informed him. The pup, cradled in Red's arms, regarded the officer with soulful eyes and certainly seemed happy with its new masters.

"O.K., O.K.," agreed the Officer of the Day, himself a dog-lover, as he tweaked the pup's ear, "but remember this has got to hold you guys for awhile. We got two ducks and a ruddy Angora rabbit for'd now. We don't want a bigger menagerie on board than we got."

Bunker, still in his late puppyhood, was getting saltier every day. He loved to play and the rougher the play the better he liked it. The guncrew were his gods and he followed them faithfully. They were teaching him new tricks and he was already showing a tendency to growl

64

alarmingly at gold lace, much to the amusement of the officers.

Teatime, at four o'clock, roused the hands to mess. Shortly afterwards the buzz went round that the Captain was coming back. All eyes of those on deck watched the approaching motorboat and the figure in the stern of it bringing the news. In their regard was all the tenseness of hopeful anticipation.

Most of them hoped for a night in harbour. That would mean shore leave and all that went with it. If they couldn't have a night in, they hoped at least for a quiet night, patrolling some coastal sector which would not necessitate Action Stations and allow one watch below at a time. They hoped against hope that it would not be another night on offensive patrol off the enemy coast. These were all right in their way but when they occurred night after night the ship's company became a bit bleary-eyed. Offensive operations off the enemy coast meant that all hands would go to Action Stations about 10:30 p.m. at night and stay at Action Stations until after dawn. On these occasions sleep became so rare that it was like a memory, something which used to happen in the past.

The seaboat came alongside and the Captain climbed up the ladder and went to his quarters. Within a matter of minutes the buzz spread round the ship. Their worst fears were realized. It was "Operation Tunnel", said the buzz.

The navy's humour is evidenced in the nomenclature of operations such as this. "Tunnel" meant an offensive sweep up and down off the enemy channel coast. The callsigns given to the ships on these occasions carried this sense of humour still further. Tonight *Haida* was to be known as "Nuzzle", *Athabaskan* was "Chummy" and *Huron* had some name like "Ducky".

65

"Cooks to the galley" was piped early, confirming the buzz, and hands went to supper at half past five. The time for sleeping and relaxation was over now. Throughout the ship there was a quiet feeling of preparation against the night that was approaching. This was the final harbour hour.

"Special sea duty men" was piped at fifteen minutes to seven. Ten minutes later came "Hands fall in" and the waiting was over. Each division lined up in its place on deck. Up to the bridge went the Captain, dressed in his seagear. It was time to go.

A quiet command and the mooring to the buoy was slipped. As the ship swung, obedient to her engines and rudder, and started to turn down harbour, the seaboat, which had sheered off, was run alongside by her coxswain and was hooked onto the long rope falls hanging down from the davits. The moment she was attached the command was given to hoist away and the seaboat was swung up clear of the water and hoisted until she was up to the top of the davits. As her crew climbed out onto the maindeck the davits were swung inboard and the boat secured against them by heavy canvas bands and snugged down. By that time the ship had completed her turn and was headed down harbour.

It was always an interesting passage · going out. In the narrow waterway the shores were very close and one could see everything that was going on. Many people were walking and girls would stop and wave to the lads in the outbound ships.

"There's the Killick's bit of squash," whispered Red to the seaman on his left, talking out of the corner of his mouth in order to preserve the illusion that he was properly standing at ease as the ship went down harbour.

66

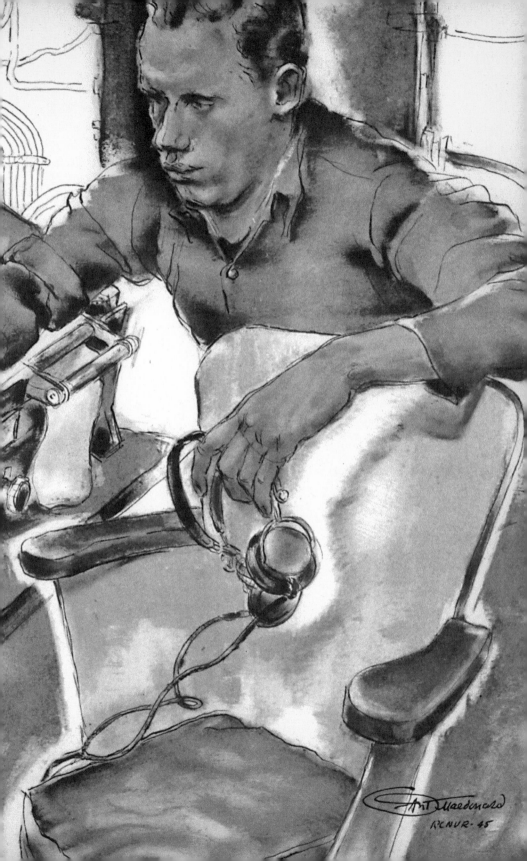

"WHAT'S THE BUZZ?"

"Not the little dark one with the figure?" came the answering whisper.

"Sure," said Red. "That's her all right. She saw the Killick up in the Dockyard and she's been writing love-letters to him ever since. She goes for him in a big way. One of these times she'll mail them."

The remark, as was intended, reached the Killick's ears. He grinned, but somewhat self-consciously, and his eyes strained sideways for a good look. As became the Bluenose tradition he attempted to maintain a dignified silence about such matters but he took a certain pride in Red's teasing on that score. He was a big, upstanding lad and he felt that if a woman looked at him twice it was, after all, a very natural thing.

"There's Sally," whispered Red's mate excitedly and his hand went up almost involuntarily in a wave that stopped halfway as he realized the P.O.'s eye was on him and the Gunnery Officer was looking in his direction too.

"Take it easy Joe," whispered Red.

"We're going to get married when this one pays off," whispered Joe proudly. "I asked her old man after I asked Sally. She wanted me to. He's all for it an' wants me to come into the garage business with him after I get through."

Red winked and concentrated his attention then on the people looking at them from the beach roadway. These people knew ships and they always looked longer and more closely when they saw the Tribals go out. There was a grim, purposeful look about these ships that heartened the on-lookers and brought a lift to their heads and a light to their eyes. They couldn't imagine fighting craft like these wasting time or motion on irrelevant matters.

For the shoreside people it was the evening hour, the time for relaxation, for social obligations and all the things that people do of an evening. For the lean Tribals which they watched slipping seaward however there would be no friendly pubs or firesides this night. For them there would be just the darkness under the stars off the enemy coast, the darkness that could hide so many things, not the least of which was death.

The ship was passing the signal station, a low, flatroofed structure perched on a hilltop with mast and yards and flashing signal lamps. All hands came to attention as the pipe for "Still" sounded and then stood easy as they went swiftly past. Here they would be reported as having officially sailed from the inner harbour.

Drake's Island came abeam on the starboard hand. On the other side they could see the crowds taking the air on Plymouth Hoe, stopping to look down at the four Tribals reaching down towards the seagate in line ahead.

The wind was freshening now as they neared the seagate, blowing in from the open channel seas outside. Over to port, behind the anti-submarine net, the waiting cruiser slipped her moorings and turned to accompany them out.

Clear of the seagate and looking back they caught their last glimpse of the harbour. The sun was setting to the westward of the old city, lighting rooftops and windows with the last banners of the day. Ahead were the darkening seas of the Channel. Shrilly the pipe whistled again: "Port Watch to Defence Stations."

The night's work had begun and they were too busy now to think of what they had left behind. Guns and firing circuits were checked and tested. From X gundeck came the thump-thump of the pompom as it opened fire and then the Oerlikon gunners spotting the bursts of the pompom shells in the evening skies, opened fire at them with tracer.

"Darken Ship" was piped and every man off duty headed below to get what rest he could while the deadlights were screwed down on portholes, hatches closed and thick canvas

68

blackout curtains drawn into place across all hatches and doorways opening on deck. Action Stations would be sounded at half past ten, if no enemy contact was made before that. From then on the whole ship's company would be on duty all night. There would be no relief until after dawn.

Few slept as the ships of Force 26 sailed southwards across the Channel towards the French Coast. Most of the hands preferred to relax with their thoughts. Each man had his own.

In Halifax it would be afternoon now but out on the far Pacific Slope it would still be morning. At this hour the homes in the cities, town and villages of far-off Canada seemed very close. This was the heart's quiet hour, the mind's farewell to home and the remembered faces that were dear, the last long thoughts against the things which might be in the night that was upon them.

"Give me a hand chum," said the Westerner to Red as he attempted to get a lammy coat over his big lifejacket. Ten o'clock had passed and the watch below were rousing and struggling into their action gear in preparation for the Action Stations call at ten-thirty. Heavy underwear, thick socks, sweaters, lifejackets, ear protectors, anti-flash hoods, steel helmets, lammy coats and other paraphernalia were being assembled and put on. It made them appear unduly bulky but had the advantage of being easily peeled in a sudden emergency.

Bunker, in a fever of puzzled excitement, was nuzzling around attempting to understand these preparations. When the cocoa and sandwiches came down he was too interested to pay any attention to food and Red admonished him to stay in his "mick" and keep out of trouble. They had fashioned a small hammock for him and promised he would

69

have a lifejacket and steel helmet just as soon as they could find time to get around to it.

"Here we go boys," said the Killick studying his watch. As he spoke the buzzers sounded their insistent clamour throughout the ship.

Bunker, showing signs of open mutiny, refused to stay in the Mess as the hands tumbled out to the first darkness of the decks. Red grabbed him and handed him over to a hurrying Communications Rating.

"Keep him in the T.S. (Transmitting Station) chum," he requested. "He'll be out of harm there."

Along the decks running figures were moving with the swiftness of long practice to their stations. Magazine hatches were quickly opened and manned by ammunition supply parties. Fire-control squads closed hatches to sections which would not be in use and the ship was swiftly and surely readied for instant action.

Up to the bridge, where the Captain, Action Officer of the Watch. Gunnery, Torpedo, Observer officers and signalmen were alert and ready, came a steady stream of reports as every action station in the ship reported manned and ready.

It was quiet up on the open bridge under the stars. Visibility was good, about two miles. There was no moon. *Haida*, with *Athabaskan* close astern, formed the starboard sub-division of Force 26. Over to port the cruiser *Black Prince* could be discerned and beyond, screening her on the other side, *Huron* and *Ashanti* formed the port sub-division.

The steady bridge watch was maintained in silence. Force 26 was nearing the French Coast and officers, signalmen and lookouts kept sweeping the seas and the skies through their binoculars, alert for a flicker of light, an untoward movement or the sound of aircraft.

Two hours passed without incident and then, at one

70

o'clock, a shore light was sighted and plotted. Ten minutes later a shore searchlight was noted, directed straight up. "Must be looking for planes," remarked the Navigator.

At twenty-five minutes past one the flash of gunfire was observed from shore batteries but no fall of shot could be seen near the silent, speeding ships. A few minutes later another shorelight and further flashes were sighted and the Senior Officer in the cruiser ordered a slight alteration of course off the land.

This had just been done when a signal was received which brought immediate alertness. The cruiser had picked up radar echoes dead ahead. The echoes appeared to be ships and were coming directly towards Force 26. A few minutes later the radar contacts were confirmed by each of the four Tribals. There were four or five echoes and they appeared to be turning away now. The time was ten minutes past two.

"Increase speed to 28 knots" came a signal from the S.O. (Senior Officer) in the cruiser and Force 26 revved up engines. Two minutes later another order came to increase speed again and the ships increased revolutions until they were making 30 knots. The turbines hummed to a higher note and the Plot reported to the Bridge that the enemy contacts, which appeared to be destroyers, were being held now and closed.

CHAPTER VI

From Senior Officer Force 26 to Destroyers: Increase to maximum speed to close and engage the enemy.

The sharp crack of the cruiser's guns broke the darkness as she opened fire with starshell to illuminate the enemy. *Haida* increased speed and the hum of her turbines rose to a high eerie whine as she raced through the seas, with *Athabaskan* keeping station right astern.

The cruiser's role in the opening stages of this type of engagement was to provide illumination while the destroyers closed in to engage. *Haida's* bridge crew watched intently for the starshell to burst. It seemed like an interminable moment until the bursts showed and the starshell illuminated an area of sea to the right of the bearing of the enemy ships. Nothing was visible.

"More left . . . more left," signalled *Haida* and the cruiser corrected and fired again. Once again there was a long tense moment and then the starshell burst again, flooding the horizon above the indicated bearing with sudden light.

"There they are, there they are!" came half a dozen voices. Low down on the horizon, five miles ahead, several little dark objects could be seen under the spread of starshell.

"Three, possibly four enemy destroyers, making to Eastward under cover of smokescreen," reported the observers. The time was twenty-six minutes past two.

"Open fire!" said the Captain.

"Commence! Commence! Commence!" came the call to the guns.

Within thirty seconds there was a crash and the acrid smell of cordite mingled with the night air as *Haida* opened

72

"EACH MAN HAD HIS OWN THOUGHTS."

fire with A and B mountings and the ship heeled with the recoil.

The Officer of the Watch, the Starboard Observer and a signalman held their ears and opened their mouths. The moment the blast was over they reached hurriedly for a piece of cotton wool to stuff into their ears. They had made this trip so many times without incident that this time they were caught short.

Others, among whom were two of the torpedo crew, hearing the roar of heavy gunfire for the first time, didn't quite know what to do about it until the Torpedo Gunner's Mate pushed some cotton wool at them and gruffly remarked that they couldn't stand around holding their ears all the time.

The track of the four shells from *Haida's* two forward mountings could be followed plainly, as they were all tracer type ammunition. The bridge crew watched, tense and expectant as the shells arched across the night skies and glanced down towards the enemy ships, seeming to go more swiftly near the targets.

The cruiser was firing steadily and so were *Haida, Huron, Ashanti* and *Athabaskan*. Now came answering flashes from the guns of the German ships and starshell burst along the night horizon away over to port. The enemy ships were evidently bewildered and were seeking to locate the guns which had lashed at them so suddenly out of the night.

Force 26 maintained its formation and swept on in pursuit of the enemy. It was a pleasant surprise to discover that the German destroyers, which were reputed to be much faster than the Tribals, were evidently unable to draw away and the range was actually being closed.

It was a stern chase to the Eastward. *Haida* was abeam the enemy's smoke screen now. It was a light whitish colour

73

and was about a hundred feet high and some five hundred yards off on the starboard side.

As the guns of Force 26 thundered continuously and sent a steady stream of missiles ahead of them towards the enemy the searching German starshells found the bearing of the outer sub-division. *Huron* and *Ashanti* and the whole area between the speeding ships were illuminated by their greenish, ghostly brilliance.

"A hit! A hit!" came the cry as a glow of flame was seen to burst for a moment on an enemy ship and show through the smoke screen. A few moments later the cry came again as a hit was spotted on another enemy ship. And still, as the Tribals raced along all out, the range was slowly but inexorably decreasing.

Then the illumination over the enemy ships, which had been splendid up to now, suddenly died and there was only darkness up ahead. From the cruiser came a short signal that her B gun turret was out of action and could fire no more starshell. As the port sub-division were fouling her line of fire the cruiser checked her guns and sheered seaward to clear herself.

Two minutes later her lookouts sighted a torpedo approaching and her Captain ordered Hard Aport. The torpedo passed up the starboard side. More enemy torpedoes were observed and, as her B turret was still out of action and the cruiser's role was definitely restricted to supplying illumination and keeping to seaward in these circumstances, she now disengaged to the Northward. The time was forty-eight minutes past two.

Command of the destroyers now devolved upon the Captain of *Haida* and, following their prearranged plan, illumination was provided by the second destroyer in each of the two sub-divisions. This permitted the two leading destroyers, *Haida* and *Huron*, to maintain their fire upon the

74

enemy ships from both forward mountings on each ship. *Athabaskan,* close astern on *Haida's* starboard quarter, fired starshell from her B mounting and *Ashanti* provided a similar service for *Huron.* Both the following destroyers utilized their A mountings to engage the enemy also.

At a minute past three two enemy destroyers were observed to emerge to windward of their smokescreen and then turn back into it again. It was appreciated by *Haida* that this move had been made to fire torpedoes and all ships in Force 26 were immediately warned. *Haida's* bridge watch observed the starshell-lit waters ahead of them with care.

"E Boat at Red two five," called the Officer of the Watch, and every eye on deck looked immediately towards that bearing. Their shore training before going to sea had familiarized every man with the simple bearing identification system. The starboard side of a fighting ship from bow to stern numbers the visible horizon on that side from one to one hundred and eighty degrees. As the starboard side is always Green and the port side always Red, an object abeam on the starboard side at right angles to the bridge would be Green 90. An object midway between the bow and the bridge would be Green four five.

The same system applies on the port side, except that any object on the port side is always preceded by the word Red, indicating it is on that side. When the shout of Red two five was passed along the decks every man immediately looked twenty-five degrees off the port bow.

A fast-moving object, putting up a wide bow wave about four or five feet in height, could be seen approaching on an opposite course directly off the port bow. No sign of any superstructure could be seen on it in the light of the enemy starshell over that area, and it swept past *Haida's* port side, about four hundred yards off, being lost to sight then as the starshell which illuminated it dropped into the sea. It could have been a surface torpedo or a small, extremely fast motor torpedo boat.

Following the contour of the coastline as close in as was safe, *Haida* and *Athabaskan* found themselves racing ahead in close proximity to the enemy's smoke screen. As the coastline veered to the south in this area the two inside destroyers, *Haida* and *Athabaskan*, were drawing ahead of *Huron* and *Ashanti*. All the Tribals were making the same speed but the inside ships, like the inside horses on a race-track, had the advantage of position. The two destroyers to seaward had farther to travel.

Heavy fire was arching over the smokescreen from some point inshore, seemingly directed towards *Huron* and *Ashanti* as it was passing well over *Haida* and *Athabaskan*. All four Tribals were directing a furious crescendo of fire against the enemy ships ahead and the action, destroyers against destroyers now in equal numbers, was reaching a furious tempo as the sweating gunners served their quick-firing charges.

A minefield was known to be in this area but the German ships fled right through it and the Tribals followed them with grim determination. The shooting from the landward side was far astern now and seemed to have died away. Up ahead were the islands of Sept Iles, their shores dangerously close. Tense and alert, *Haida's* bridge crew watched for some new move on the part of the German ships as it was anticipated they would now attempt to break off the engagement.

The enemy had been making their smoke screen with smoke floats and as the Tribals raced in pursuit those could be seen at regular intervals, smoke pouring from them and being carried back in the wind. Farther ahead the smoke screen looked as if it might be more irregular and, as the bridge crew watched, they caught a glimpse of something at the edge of the smokescreen ahead of them that might be a

76

ship attempting to double back. It was a momentary glimpse and was followed by a pause in which no starshell fell in that area.

To provide illumination over the suspected ship *Haida* immediately altered course to allow her X gun mounting to fire starshell. Well-aimed, the first burst was directly over and behind the target and it was fully revealed.

Streaking out clear of the smokescreen and very much closer now was a German destroyer attempting to double back. Every detail of her long hull with its high foredeck was clearly visible in the light of that well-placed starshell and the silhouette was unmistakable to eyes which had studied enemy ship silhouettes for so long.

"Elbing Class destroyer," reported the observers confidently and *Haida's* guns swung and steadied on the new target.

The bridge crew watched intently as the drama of the moment was unfolded before them in the eerie light of the starshell. One moment she was in plain view, speeding along and apparently unmarked, then *Haida's* guns crashed with salvo after salvo.

The first salvo was a direct hit, a terrible blow that caught the Elbing right amidships, about ten feet below her maindeck, and crumpled through her plates as if they were paper to go on and explode inside. Another crashed in aft, below deck level again, then one went in below the bridge and another smashed into her just abaft the first.

Results showed immediately. Great geysers of steam rose from the enemy destroyer's midships section and she slowed and stopped dead in her tracks. Red tongues of flame licked hungrily upwards from where the first salvo had gone home and showed above her maindeck. From where the second and third salvos had struck home, aft and forward of the first hit, came other leaping tongues of flame and the

77

three fires joined rapidly to make a blazing inferno of her maindeck.

Athabaskan was firing now and hitting her too. A salvo smashed through the high bows and then another, and fires broke out there also until only the upper bridge and her afterdeck still showed black in the sea of fire which was engulfing her.

Across the flame-lit expanse of water between them and the burning ship, only two and a half miles away, the bridge watch on *Haida* could hear the roar and hiss of her escaping steam loudly and clearly as, followed by *Athabaskan,* they closed in for the kill.

To seaward and ahead of them, *Huron* and *Ashanti,* having lost sight of the enemy ships which they had been pursuing, turned around and came back to get in on the battle.

Survivors could be seen attempting to get clear of the burning Elbing on a liferaft but her guns were still being served and *Haida* had no alternative. A salvo, intended to strike below the waterline, crashed into the enemy's hull and sent raft and occupants hurtling skyward in a shower of debris.

Her guns appeared to be silenced then. There was only the roar and crackle of the flames and small, intermittent explosions. Circling like Indians, their silhouettes showing like black shadows against the firelit horizon, the grim Tribals sailed round her, close in.

Still some fanatics lived aboard the doomed enemy destroyer. As the Tribals passed, some four hundred yards off, two streams of tracer spat with unexpected suddenness from points high on her bridge and far back on her quarterdeck. Streaking across the narrow gap, it swept along *Haida's* after superstructure, spattered *Athabaskan's* length and beat a devil's tattoo on *Huron's* bridge.

Immediately the close-range guns of the Tribals went into

78

"THE GUN CREWS WATCHED HER GO."

action with a swift effective answer. A stream of coloured tracer spat from *Haida's* Oerlikons and swept the enemy's decks, probing and ricochetting over her bridge and after-structure. The Elbing didn't fire any more.

Still she floated. Burning, aflame from bow to stern now, she seemed unsinkable and the Tribals closed again. Salvo after salvo rocked into her, smashing into the hull and sending up showers of sparks against the black masses of oily smoke billowing to leeward of the doomed Elbing.

Then, as they watched, she rolled to port. Her bows dipped, she slipped swiftly under the sea and the darkness closed down. From *Haida's* foredeck came the sound of hoarse cheering as the gun crews watched her go. The time was twenty minutes past four.

Flashing their fighting lights the Tribals formed up and stood away to seaward on course for England. The stars came out again and the night wind was fresh and sweet on blackened faces and nostrils after the reek of cordite. The damaged enemy ships had probably got into some adjacent protected port on the French Coast. They would have to be left for another night. Dawn was near and it was time to go.

As *Haida* sped back towards Plymouth damage to the ship was checked by the First Lieutenant. There were several splinter holes through the hull and X gundeck; the Sick Bay and the Captain's day cabin, which was an emergency operating theatre during Action Stations, had been swept by close-range fire.

Several men had suffered wounds, all of a minor nature. The most serious had been sustained by an officer, who had been unaware that he was wounded and had been asking how come his boots were soaking wet when he discovered it was blood, not salt water, which was oozing from them. Red proudly exhibited a grazed arm and Joe, the lad who

79

intended to marry Sally, had a dented helmet and a bump on the head to show for his night's work.

Dawn came up over the Channel seas and found the ships of Force 26 well on their homeward way. No enemy planes were in sight and soon the welcome sound of the quarter-master's pipe and the command "Secure Action Stations" was heard along the decks. The long night was over and the tired guncrews and supply parties went below to take off their heavy seagear and relax. As the ship would be entering harbour in an hour or so and every man who could be up was anxious to be on deck when she did so, few of them attempted to sleep. Sitting around, they waited for breakfast. The cruiser had rejoined and was leading Force 26 back to harbour.

CHAPTER VII

Destroyers will berth alongside to make good action damage, replenish magazines and prepare for sea. Haida and Athabaskan to go to half-hour notice for steam at 1600.

"Have you any casualties or survivors?"

The now familiar hail which presaged their arrival was answered, for the first time, in the affirmative. Through the seagate they came with their battle ensign, the white ensign fluttering at the yard signifying they had just come from action.

Sailing up harbour they were the subject of interested scrutiny. The buzz had got around, in the mysterious way it does in naval ports, and ship after ship saluted them. The ship's company were happy. They had done something and they felt their ship had gained prestige in this action. They were very proud of *Haida*. She had acquitted herself well.

Ambulances were at the dock to take off the wounded, and numerous visitors, from the Commander-in-Chief down, were waiting to come aboard. They had made a good showing and everyone was pleased.

Dockyard mateys swarmed aboard to patch the holes which enemy fire had made in the hull and fix up fittings which the vibration of high speed, combined with the effect of the prolonged fire of the ship's own guns, had shaken loose. The for'd messdecks, under A and B gun mountings, looked like a shambles. Steam radiators had shaken off their bulkhead fixings and fallen over. Chunks of asbestos had dropped from overhead pipes and many of these were sagging low. Crockery, breaking loose from lashed cupboards, lay broken on the decks and seagear was scattered everywhere. It was quite a mess to clean up, though only minor damage.

Replenishing magazines was a heavy chore. Approximately two thousand one hundred rounds of all types of ammunition had been expended, more than half from the main gun mountings. All this had to be replaced and stored in the proper magazines.

It was a job that could only be done by hand. A covered ammunition lighter came alongside with the ammunition packed in special watertight cases. A long line of men was then formed from the barge to the magazines two decks below and each shell was passed from hand to hand. They were heavy and had to be handled with care, high explosive being what it is, and the job took time.

Four o'clock found the ship ready, however, except for a few minor things such as the starboard motor cutter, still riddled from enemy close-range fire. Hands went to supper early and at seven o'clock *Haida* and *Athabaskan* slipped their lines and stood down harbour to sea. *Huron* and *Ashanti*, having suffered more extensive damage, would be held in port for four or five days yet, as the opportunity was being taken to boiler-clean them during this period.

Large-scale amphibious exercises with landing craft of several types were under way along the Channel coast and, with every seaworthy destroyer that could be spared in the Command, the two Tribals were being used to patrol to seaward of the operation in a given sector.

Both crews hoped for a quiet night and it turned out not too badly. Action Stations were sounded on three occasions: E boats were suspected in the vicinity and, although the alarms came to nothing, their presence was verified later when news came that a supply craft had been torpedoed and sunk twenty miles away in the next area.

When morning came they returned to harbour, anchored

82

in the outer waters for a while and then went up to refuel and go to their buoy off Flagstaff again. They were getting to know that particular buoy rather well. It had come to be home to them.

Here visitors were waiting for every mess on the ship. The *Prince Robert,* Canada's anti-aircraft cruiser, was in with a convoy from the Med, and every man aboard wanted the news of the engagement at first hand.

Gunnery actions have a particular fascination for navymen. *Haida* had been lucky having a target pop out in front of her and every phase of the engagement was recounted again. Up in the messdecks a visitor, having learned all he could of the action, turned to other matters of interest.

"What about the reindeer you guys brought down from Russia?" he asked. "What happened to it?"

Dan the Westerner answered, after looking casually around to see who was in the vicinity and noting with satisfaction the presence of a cook.

"The reindeer. Yeah, that was very sad. You know that was a good reindeer when it come aboard, just full of life.

"We took some feed on for it, that sphagnum moss stuff that goes for grass up there and the first coupla days it did all right. It did too good for it ate up all the moss. We tried it with our grub then but it just took one whiff and then shied away shaking its head. Wouldn't touch it. All it would eat was a package of chewing gum one of the boys gave it.

"We asked the Cox'n what to do and he asked the Jimmy. Well the Jimmy thought it over and reckoned it was up to the cooks. He had enough trouble on his hands figuring how he would ever get a chance to paint the ship, so we turned it over to them. We got some right smart cooks here and it was a kind of challenge to them."

"How did they do?" asked the "Robert" man.

83

"Oh they did their best. They chopped up cabbage and some other stuff and made it look as much like that moss as they could and then they put it down in front of the reindeer.

"That old reindeer was gettin' pretty hungry by then. He nuzzled it and guzzled it. Ate the whole bunch."

"He went for it?" asked a listener.

"Sure he went for it. How was the poor dumb animal to know what he was up against? I can see him now. He gives a sigh and shakes his head kinda puzzled like; then his eyes roll up and go right out of sight. His insides shook like they were depth-charged and he rolls over, dead before he hit the deck."

"Pusser grub!" commented the visitor.

"Yeah, pusser grub," confirmed the seaman, "it would kill a horse."

"It hasn't killed you yet," interjected the cook, stung to a reply.

"Give it time, give it time," rejoined the seaman, "if it wasn't for the parcels I get from my mother and the dope from the Sick Bay I'd 'a been a stiff long ago."

"Did you bury it at sea?" asked the visitor.

"We did and we didn't. Some of it was there when we buried it, bits like the hoofs and the horns. I'm not saying who done it, but I heard the buzz. The cooks and the stokers ate steak that night and they say there was some in the wardroom too. There's no tellin' what some people will eat," he concluded sorrowfully, just as a Leading Hand looked into the mess.

"There's no telling when you'll eat again, cowboy," remarked that worthy, "unless you get crackin'. The seaboat's crew was piped five minutes ago and you're it. Get going."

The gang stood aside respectfully, almost reverently, as he departed. This was a yarn spinner of no mean calibre.

Loud laughter from the foredeck brought half the hands

84

Grant Macdonald
RCNVR ·45

"WE GOT SOME RIGHT SMART COOKS HERE."

in the messdecks out to see what the amusement was about. Red was leaning over the rail with a suspicious air of serene contentment. Right up forward stood a pot of white paint, conspicuously unattended, not a rating standing within fourteen feet of it. Half the men on deck were looking over the rail at something in the water and the other half were being amused by the spectacle of Able Seaman Bunker.

Excited by the laughter, he was prancing around trying to understand why none of them would let him put his paws up on their legs. Both forepaws were a beautiful shade of pusser white, made so by the fact that he had stepped into the paint pot. There were also a couple of white patches on his hindquarters.

A look over the rail set the newcomers laughing heartily also and explained the unattended paintpot. The buoy to which the ship was moored was becoming very familiar to the ship's company. They seemed to be getting sent there every time they came in, much to their disgust, as they preferred to be alongside one of the jetties.

When night leave is granted a seaman has no difficulty returning to a ship which is alongside a jetty but when the ship is at a buoy in the stream it is a different proposition. The last liberty boat leaves the shore at midnight and, unless latecomers are lucky enough to get a lift out from some passing harbour craft, there is no return until the liberty boat comes in again at seven in the morning, in time to get all hands back before leave expires at seven thirty a.m.

Red or some other humorist had expressed his feelings in no uncertain manner, as a glance over the side quickly revealed. Painted in large white letters on the buoy to which the ship was moored were the words "CANADA HOUSE".

Athabaskan was alongside and late in the afternoon a heavy consignment of mail, parcels and cigarettes from

85

Canada reached the ships. Time went fast then until seven o'clock brought the order to slip.

It had been a good day, a day of sunshine and good company. The ships would have preferred a night in to get caught up on sleep, but war knows only its exigencies so it was grumble and go. Coastal Forces minelaying craft would be operating inshore in French waters and the two Tribals were being sent to cover them to seaward.

Haida slipped first, turned around and stood down harbour. *Athabaskan* had a little trouble getting clear and scraped Number Six Buoy as she swung around. This caused her to lose distance and she increased speed down harbour to catch up. At the seagate, *Haida* slowed to pass through. *Athabaskan* had been travelling fast to catch up and she slowed now to maintain station.

Down on the quarterdeck a group of officers was talking. A Lieutenant, looking back at *Athabaskan,* said she'd be lucky, she'd get back all right. He had a premonition of trouble and figured *Haida,* being leading ship, would collect anything that was going.

"Should be more than two of us," grumbled another, not realizing that the job was a straight covering patrol to seaward of the Coastal Forces minelayers and the ship would probably be twenty miles off the French Coast all night and wouldn't have to go in.

Sailors of course would *natter* if the whole Home Fleet was with them, regarding it as part of their privilege.

Action Stations, delayed by the Captain until midnight to allow the crew as much rest as possible, brought all hands tumbling out for the night.

The moon was still up and would not go down for another two hours yet. The ship was ghosting along on a moonlit sea, in a deceptive light that was not approved by her company. Better the darkness than this, for destroyers. This

86

was E boat weather. The bigger ships could be seen too easily from a long way off.

It was a strange-looking moon and atmospherics were curiously freaky tonight, as the ship's instruments were revealing. Off from the moon the night skies were filled with stars, some of them so low that they looked like lights on the surface of the distant waters.

Athabaskan, reflecting the moonlight and looking like a ship of silver as she cruised astern, was plainly visible. Like *Haida* she was in the first degree of readiness.

Up on the bridge *Haida's* captain stood by himself, his binoculars ready to his hands. On his right, head and shoulders silhouetted in the moonlight as he stood on the raised platform behind the compass, was the Officer of the Watch. On him was the responsibility for the maintenance of the ship's proper course and speed. Vigilant and alert, he followed the course. The Gunnery Officer, telephone headset strapped to his chest and in constant communication with the guns and the director control tower where the rangefinding crew were housed, awaited orders.

Behind the Officer of the Watch, muffled in his sheepskin and seated on his stool with his array of telephones before him, was the Illumination Control Officer. His job was to direct the firing of starshell. At the order from the Captain he could illuminate the required bearing and range. Near him was the Torpedo Officer, ready to set and send his lethal messengers of death speeding at any enemy target.

At the Captain's elbow was the Yeoman of Signals, the tiny-crowsfeet around his keen eyes showing his calling. At other points on the silent bridge were other officers and ratings. In the wings, binoculars on their swivel mounts constantly to their eyes were the lookouts.

The first hour went by, then the second and the third, the time dragging slowly. Down in the Plot below the bridge lifejacketted officers and men kept track of the ship's position and advised the bridge. Isolated though the two ships were a constant flow of signals picked up from bases and other ships kept them advised what was happening up and down Channel. Anything in which the Captain might be interested was passed to him immediately. At intervals he would come down to the Plot, study the chart and read the signal logs himself.

At three o'clock an officer from the bridge came aft looking around and stopped to have a cup of coffee with the Surgeon Lieutenant in Sick Bay.

"Quiet night so far," he informed the Surgeon. "We're about twenty miles off Ile de Bas. Should be turning for home soon and I'll be glad when we do. I've had a hunch of trouble all night. Still, it's not likely anything will happen now," he added.

Hardly had he finished speaking when the engines revved up to a higher speed and the telephone rang. The hands of the clock were at twenty minutes past three.

"Stand by," came the command. "We're closing the coast." "O.K.," acknowledged the officer and ran forward.

In the wardroom and mess flats the supply parties, who had been lying down fully dressed, got to their feet and disappeared down into the magazine hatches, ready for what might come. The damage-control parties picked up their gear and stood by their pumps. In the Sick Bay the Surgeon checked over his equipment again and noted that everything was in place.

Up in the Plot officers worked swiftly as they studied a signal which had just been received. Night radar reconnaissance had discovered two enemy destroyers with a third craft, possibly an E boat, making to the Westward, close in on the French Coast.

The Captain had decided to steam on an intercepting

88

course and close in on them. As his ships would be at the western end of their area at the point of intersection, he hoped to turn the enemy and drive them Eastwards along the coast. By achieving this he would prevent them escaping to the Westward and so round the corner to Brest and, at the same time give himself the full benefit of the operational area in which he was engaged.

Less than forty-eight hours since their last action and now the chance had come again. Heeling over as they turned, the two lean Tribals settled swiftly on the new course and angled in towards the French shore. Every man in the ships was on the *qui vive* now and alert. The odds might be against them and the Coastal Force minelaying craft, which had been re-called and were now on their way home, could furnish no assistance in a scrap like the one now shaping up. On the speed of their own hands and brains would rest the outcome.

CHAPTER VIII

Have made contact with two enemy ships and am closing to engage.

The moon had gone down as the ships closed the land but there was a slight coastal haze which made observation difficult. Information coming up from the Plot gave the range of the enemy ships as 7,000 yards now.

"Ignite," said the Captain.

"Three stars, spreading left, fire!" ordered the Illumination Control Officer through his telephone, and the guns at X mounting fired with a crack like a whip as the ship sped onwards.

"There they are . . . two of them."

"Red five o, two enemy destroyers," called an observer.

"Open fire," said the Captain.

Haida's for'd gun mountings came into action then and the ship rolled with the recoil. *Athabaskan* was firing too, with starshell and main armament.

"Enemy making smoke and turning to Eastward," came a report.

The Captain studied the situation briefly. It was a critical moment. If he turned too soon the enemy might still get past to the Westward. Deciding to take a chance on that he gave the order.

"Port 20, executive to Athabaskan." The two Tribals heeled over as they started to come around, maintaining their fire at the same time. Binoculars glued to their eyes, observers studied the smudges in the enemy smokescreen from which his gunflashes were coming. Enemy starshell was bursting over and between them and the whistle of other

"EVERY MAN WAS ON THE *QUI VIVE* NOW."

shells passing overhead could be heard as he brought his main armament into action.

Just then there came a cry, "Athabaskan's been hit," which made every head on *Haida's* bridge turn around.

They could see her plainly. She was right on station, close astern, and had not yet lost her way. From somewhere aft of the bridge, a great column of flame was shooting up, outlining her foresection in bold relief. Even as they looked her B gun fired.

From the enemy ships there came a frenzied burst of gunfire as they sighted the burning destroyer and turned all their guns on her in an endeavour to give her a knockout blow.

His face grim, the Captain of *Haida* spoke briefly. "Make smoke," he ordered; "we'll put a screen across to protect Athabaskan. Tell them what we're doing," he added.

Telephones jangled to engineroom and afterdeck. As the ship swung to starboard a stoker crawled out on the afterdeck. Braving the blast from Y guns he reached up and opened the valve which turned on the chemical smoke producers. They worked immediately and, combined with the black masses of smoke which began to pour from *Haida's* funnels, soon put a dense, shielding curtain of smoke between the stricken ship and her enemies.

In *Athabaskan,* after the crash and explosion aft there was no panic. That the propellers had ceased to function was evident and the ship was being carried forward only by her own impetus. The first report reached the bridge.

"Torpedo hit near the gearing room. Heavy damage aft the apron and Y gun collapsed. Steering gear out of action."

"Damage control party on the job?" asked the Captain.

"After pump is gone sir. The for'd pump is being taken back and rigged now."

"Try the after steering position," ordered the Captain.

91

"Better hoist out the seaboats, but don't lower them yet. Haida is making a smoke screen and will try to take us in tow later."

"Permission to clear B gun of starshell," requested the Illumination Control Officer, a veteran of the torpedoed H.M.C.S. Ottawa.

"Permission granted," said the Captain.

B gun fired. It was to be the last shot from *Athabaskan*. There was feverish activity now on the crippled ship's decks. Up for'd the bosun's party worked hurriedly to rig the towing hawser. Amidships, by the tubes, the Chief Engineer, the Gunner T, the T.G.M. and others hauled the heavy 70-ton portable pump into position and started to get it ready to deal with the rising flames behind them.

"After steering position out of action and ship settling by the stern, sir," came a report to the bridge.

The young Captain nodded. "All hands stand by their Abandon Ship stations," he said. "I'll let Haida know."

Obedient to the order the crew started to file off the bridge. A signalman's lifejacket strap was loose and an officer, checking them as they left, stopped him and tightened it up.

"Better keep that fast, son," he admonished, "you don't want it to come off in the water." The Captain remained on the bridge, watching them go.

There had been no power failure. The tubes had been swung inboard and trimmed fore and aft and down there on the maindeck the men still worked desperately to bring the pump into action. It was almost ready. The Chief Engineer turned to put the feedline overboard and the Gunner T was fixing up the fairleads to the starter when a sudden rumble in the fire presaged disaster.

A great roar of flame went blasting skywards and the

after part of the ship became a holocaust. The deck on which they stood tilted crazily and then collapsed as internal explosions blew it out. When it was over only one man of the crowd who had been working there was still alive on deck.

It was the T.G.M. He had been flung forward from where he had been working, bent over the pump. Dazed, he thought he had landed in the for'd stokehold. Somehow he staggered up again.

Great blobs of burning oil were falling everywhere, over the forward section of the maindeck and the bridge. Men standing by the boats, among whom were the bridge party, covered their heads with their arms and dashed blindly forward, trying to find shelter under the boats, away from the burning oil. Many plunged headlong into the sea.

A signalman, clutching the ship's brass telescope which he had brought down from the bridge, handed it to one of his mates who reached up and put it in the whaler. More oil came down. The ship lurched violently and most of those who were left went tumbling over the side. Up on the foredeck the same fate overtook the towing party.

"Abandon Ship!" came a shout. The T.G.M. heard it where he leaned against a davit. Reaching out his arm he attempted to grasp the rail and go over but his arm wouldn't move. Unaware that it was broken in two places and that blood was streaming from his gashed and broken head, he looked dumbly at the rail trying to comprehend the meaning of this strange fact.

The ship heeled and he sat down heavily on the deck. He felt himself sliding and lay back to stop. It was no good. Sliding on his back end, he went under the rail and into the sea. The sudden shock of the cold water revived him and he turned on his side and swam with his good arm. The ship was sinking and he knew he had to get clear of the suction. He was a strong, well-built man, in excellent condition and a good swimmer.

About fifty yards away from the ship's side he looked back. The *Athabaskan* was going. She had righted and now the bow was rising. Up, up it came until it was nearly perpendicular and the ship was clear of the surface almost back to the first funnel. She seemed to poise there a moment and then slipped swiftly backwards, down into the engulfing waters The brightness disappeared and darkness came down over the sea.

Haida, alone, and with the fire of both German destroyers converging on her, was carrying the fight to the enemy. If her gunners had been fast before, they fought desperately now. Far below them the lights in the forward magazines snapped out as a splinter hit came in somewhere overhead, but in the dim illumination of a couple of hand torches the supply parties, down on their knees in the confined magazine space, passed the heavy shells by hand and kept the guns fed until the emergency lighting came on.

"A hit." The tell-tale glow of fire broke out amidships on the first German destroyer and smouldered through the smoke. Something was happening over there. The second enemy ship appeared to be slowing and was falling behind the first. Studying the situation, the Captain decided to change targets and *Haida's* guns swung on the second enemy ship.

One salvo punched out at her; another and another, as the guns were ranged and directed, and then came a hit. High amidships flames mounted on the German's superstructure.

"It's a hit," came the relieved shout. Another salvo thudded into her and the flames spread. Then suddenly the burning enemy destroyer gave out with a vicious burst of close-range fire directed towards her fleeing consort.

It was answered by a return burst from the other ship. In the confusion they seemed unable to tell friend from foe.

A deep rumble and the noise of a tremendous explosion from somewhere astern caused *Haida's* bridge crew to look back again. They saw an awesome sight. Hundreds of feet above the black pall of the smokescreen and lighting it from above, a great column of flames and debris was shooting up into the air above where their sister ship had been.

"There goes the Athabaskan," said an officer sadly, and more than one, the tense excitement sobered by the sudden tragedy, touched his helmet in a quick, instinctive salute before turning forward again to the grim, urgent business in hand. Twelve minutes before, the *Athabaskan* had been a ship like their own, powerful and fighting. Now the motley burning blobs flung high to the skies were arching down into the smoke again, the funeral pyre of a ship and many of her company.

But here, close at hand, was the burning enemy ship. She was badly hit and *Haida,* with a double motive now, surged forward for the kill.

"Reefs ahead," sang out the Officer of the Watch.

"Port 20," said the Captain, and *Haida* heeled over and swung away from the shore. The enemy destroyer, burning furiously, had driven up on the beach out of control. Swinging round, *Haida* let her have it, again and again, to finish her off. She was well afire and intermittent explosions were bursting up through the smoke and flames when they finished.

Daylight was close, too close for a long chase after the

95

other enemy destroyers up a hostile coast. Regretting the escape of the enemy destroyer but anxious to help *Athabaskan's* survivors, *Haida* turned back towards where the *Athabaskan* had been.

The Captain checked the plot. Smoke from the screen was still drifting though it was thinner now. "Fire a starshell over that bearing," he ordered, "and let's see if there's anything left of the ship on the surface that we might bump."

B gun fired and a starshell burst over the spot where the *Athabaskan* had been. Under it the black clusters of survivors could be seen. There were three or four groups and numbers of small, separated figures. The *Athabaskan* had gone under leaving no other trace. As *Haida* closed, the flashing lights of the survivors' lifejackets could be seen more than three miles away.

Heading for the largest clusters, the Captain let the ship glide to a stop among them. "All gun crews remain at their posts," he ordered. "Every man who can be spared from other positions will go to the maindeck and help the survivors inboard. All boats which will float are to be lowered and let go without crews. All life rafts are to be dropped. We shall wait for fifteen minutes. Get as many on board as you can."

It was an eerie scene in the dim, predawn gloom. Lifejacket lights were flashing and survivors were shouting and blowing their whistles in the adjacent waters as the rafts and boats were dropped and lowered away. Inshore a red rock-buoy light was flashing. Behind that rose the low shore, a rocky promontory. Above it, farther back, a lighthouse, a structural steel tower, flashed steadily.

Her engines stopped *Haida* drifted sideways with the light wind. Survivors on the starboard side could be seen

96

"THE COXSWAIN WAS AT THE WHEEL."

and heard as they drifted along but the ship was drifting downwind faster than they could swim against it.

On the port side it was a different story. Here the wind was helping them. Lining the rail *Haida's* men encouraged them and the Captain, leaning over the bridge, called them to swim in. Some thought at first it was a German ship and were keeping off. They did not know how the battle had fared and feared that *Haida* had been sunk.

The sea was heavy with fuel oil and those who reached the ship's side were covered with it from head to foot. Few had the strength left to climb up the scramble nets or the ladders, and *Haida's* people went over the side and helped them in. On one scramble net two officers and four of *Haida's* men formed a rescue line and pulled and pushed them up. Soon rescuers and rescued alike were filthy with the thick, slippery oil. Spreading on the decks it made men flounder and fall.

It was difficult to get a grip of the survivors to bring them in. There was no hand-hold on the lifejackets. To leave their arms free the rescuers hooked themselves to the scramble nets with the clasp of their life preservers.

Haida's whaler went away. It was damaged, but it would float. The starboard motor cutter was not lowered. It had been shot full of holes two nights previously and there had been no time to repair it.

The port cutter was serviceable however and three of *Haida's* men, a Leading Seaman, an Able Seaman, and a Stoker, manned it, although they knew the ship could not wait for them. Clearing the falls, the Coxswain took his position and directed the stoker at the engine with his whistle, as if it was a routine trip, and they turned away from the ship.

The minutes were going fast. The allotted quarter of

97

an hour had passed, by a long margin, when the call went out for the men to man their stations to get the ship under way again. From the bridge came telephone warnings at five, four, three, two and one minutes to go now, and then the ship started slowly ahead.

It was lighter now and the French coast could be plainly seen. They were off Ile de Vierge. On the starboard side of the ship a flare spluttered and burned on a dropped Carley float, lighting up the ship's side. Seizing an armful of oil-soaked survivor clothing, the only thing convenient, an officer dropped it squarely on the flare and put it out. Not until later did he learn that a survivor's carefully saved forty pounds had gone with it in an oil-soaked pair of pants.

On the port side a raft had come alongside in the final minutes. There were officers and men in it and others in the water clinging to its lifelines. "Quickly now," said a voice on deck, "the ship's getting ready to go."

"Take the wounded first," said the men on the raft, and the wounded were helped out.

It was slow work for they could not help themselves. Many were burned. The last of them were just coming up when the ship started gently ahead. She went very slowly at first, and the men on the nets worked desperately to get the survivors inboard.

From somewhere at the back of the raft a voice was heard to call, "Get away Haida, get clear." A sailor said it was the voice of the young Captain of the *Athabaskan*. Other survivors said he had swum to a raft and rested his arms on it, as if they were burned, and had encouraged them to sing.

A line parted with a snap and the raft swung away from the ship. One of the men on the net tried to hook it with his foot but missed and it drifted astern. Unaware that the raft was alongside, the bridge had ordered the ship to slow ahead, and all men back to their stations. Daylight was imminent and attack from land and air could be looked for at any moment here. It was time to go.

Unhooking themselves from the net, the rescuers scrambled up on deck, but two, on the lowest level, with the water sweeping past their legs, were unable to clear themselves and get up. An officer climbed back down and tried to free them, but the sea was catching the boom at the foot of the scramble net and sweeping over their thighs so that they had to use both hands to hang on.

Another officer lay face down on deck and attempted to haul the scramble net up clear of the water by sheer strength. He shouted for assistance but, just as the others were coming along the deck to aid him the two lads on the net were unable to maintain their hold and let go. The hooks parted at the same time and, torn loose by the seas sweeping past, they disappeared into the propeller-churned vortex of waters astern of the net.

The handful of men on deck looked after them sorrowfully. In their minds was the same dreadful thought, that the two lads might be dragged down by the suction of the powerful propellers and cut to pieces. It seemed hard that these two lads, who had taken such a courageous part in saving so many of the survivors from the *Athabaskan*, should meet this terrible fate after displaying so much heroism.

CHAPTER IX

One Elbing Class destroyer hit and driven ashore in flames near Ile de Vierge. One Elbing Class destroyer damaged escaped to Eastwards. Athabaskan torpedoed and sunk. Have picked up survivors and am returning to harbour. Request fighter protection. —Haida

The loom of dawn was coming up as *Haida* cleared the land. It was no place to linger and, as she sped swiftly seawards, every man was at his action station and lookouts searched the skies. Other destroyers, with escorting planes, were coming to meet and accompany her home, but until this covering force was met every moment in those waters held the chance of attack from air and sea. Not a single liferaft or boat was left on board. The Captain warned the ship's company the hazard from the air was particularly serious and that air attack must be expected and that they would have to fight their way home.

Below decks, in the dim light of the battle lamps, was an unforgettable sight. Survivors seemed to be everywhere in the confined quarters; in the Sick Bay, the Captain's cabin, the Officers' quarters and the messdecks.

Every blanket and sheet, lammy coat and sheepskin in the ship had been requisitioned to wrap them in. In the after flats the air reeked with the stench of fuel oil. Heaps of their soaked and useless clothing lay where it had been stripped off. Lifejackets, the oil-soaked straps slashed with bayonets to remove them, were bundled in the washrooms.

The Surgeon and his assistants worked ceaselessly among the shivering, blanket-wrapped men, administering morphine, treatment for burns and a blood transfusion for a serious case in the Captain's bunk.

100

An officer, checking the survivors' identification, was questioned repeatedly by the pathetic, oil-streaked men. They asked for their mates; they wanted to know if the ship was still fighting . . . if she was hit. The officer told them they were going home as fast as they could go, that the action was over. But even as he spoke he was listening for the sounds on deck that would intimate the expected air attack had developed.

It was cold and many of the half-frozen, water-soaked men shivered with chattering teeth as they clutched their blankets closely. All electric radiators and heating pipes had been shut off when the ship went to Action Stations to reduce the fire hazards and now, with everything battened down, all doors and ports closed and the reek of oil everywhere, not even smoking could be permitted.

"Why don't they turn on the heat . . . why can't we get a smoke?" a wounded man demanded queruously, only to be answered by a gentle shake of the head from those who listened as they tended him.

Most of the men were quiet, sincerely glad to be free of the cold, oil-covered seas. One or two of the hardier ones wanted to get up and find some clothes so that they could lend a hand. There was no fear among them, only thankfulness for their rescue and sorrow for those who had been left behind. The news of the outcome of the engagement gave them a grim satisfaction. They felt that *Haida* had avenged the *Athabaskan*.

Day broke over the gray Channel seas and showed only the lone speeding destroyer. With boats and liferafts gone, scramble nets over the side and great piles of empty shell cases lying near her ready guns she was a grim sight. But help was coming.

Far to the Northward a signal lamp flashed a quick

101

message and was answered from *Haida's* bridge. Soon the hulls of two escorting destroyers came over the horizon and took station on *Haida,* and along her decks came the welcome pipe "Secure Action Stations. Starboard watch to Defence Stations."

The long night was over. Doors and ports were opened now and the fresh salt air swept out the fumes of fuel oil. Electric heaters were switched on, steam sent through radiators and hot drinks readied for all hands. *Haida* swept on to Plymouth, her battle ensign at the upper yard arm.

She entered the seagate to find that the air-raid warning was up. Her A.A. gunners kept at their posts as she went up harbour.

Haida looked rather grimmer than usual and somewhat stripped, and she bore unmistakable evidence of having been in a scrap, but her weary crew manning their stations held their heads high. Ship after ship saluted her, their hands crowding to the rails to watch her pass. It was a good homecoming.

But it was not without its grim side. *Athabaskan* had been their "chummy ship". There had been many ties of friendship between the two crews. They had sailed together, fought together, sharing their joys and sorrows. Now *Haida* was coming in alone and the familiar ship astern wasn't with them. The *Athabaskan* would not be coming back.

Down below was a cluster of blanket-wrapped survivors and back off the French Coast were others, drifting on rafts and clinging to a few pieces of wreckage, all that remained of a good ship and her company. With them too were five of *Haida's* crew, lads who had put other lives before their own.

The ship was a mess. Great heaps of empty shell cases

102

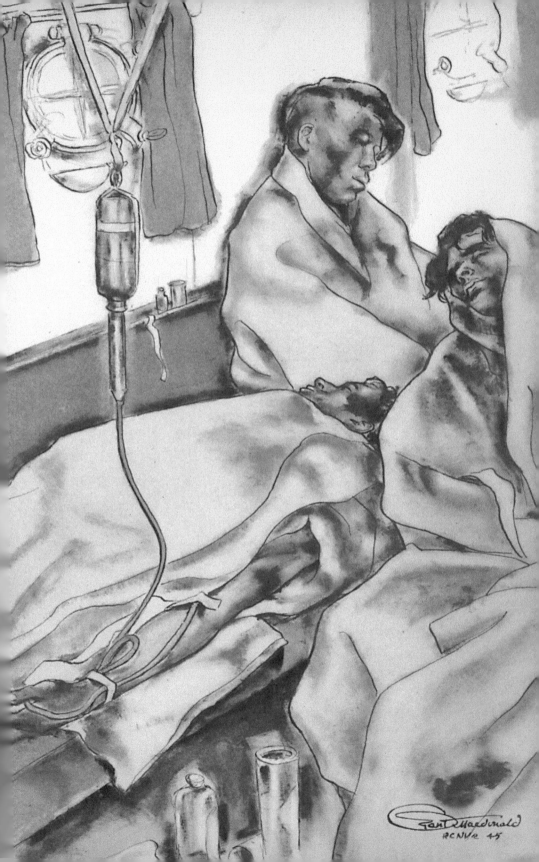

"DOWN BELOW WAS A CLUSTER OF SURVIVORS."

lay around the guns and the decks were greasy with fuel oil. All the liferafts were gone and they were left with one bullet-riddled boat. Over the rails lay the hastily pulled-in scramble nets.

Below decks it was worse. Oil was everywhere. The officers' quarters were uninhabitable and they were eating in the P.O.'s mess. All hands were tired and the loss of their comrades weighed heavily on their minds.

Nor were they looking forward to the heavy round of duties which lay before them. For as they turned wearily to the task of cleaning up their ship after landing the survivors, they knew that a much harder job was waiting to be done.

Reammunitioning is a heavy chore, particularly when more than half the ammunition has been expended and has to be made good. It is a back-bending, muscle-stretching job but it has to be done and arrangements were made to have the ammunition barge come alongside after the mid-day meal.

By noon the ship began to look as if, given time, she might be made habitable again. Her company however were dangerously close to that condition known as "out on their feet". Over them, like a nightmare, hung the knowledge that tonight they would have to go to sea again. It was the inevitable reaction over the loss of their comrades.

Chiefs, Petty Officers and Leading Seamen, upon whose shoulders the initial responsibility weighs heavily in circumstances like these, were now called upon to show the stuff that had earned them promotion. This was their job.

Not individual circumstances but the vast complex pattern of war determines what must be done. Incoming convoys, scheduled weeks before, could not be exposed to danger close to home ports because the chance of war had caused a destroyer crew to lack their sleep. Nor could lighter forces be left to face the enemy alone. When an Admiral signals that a ship must sail he does so fully cognizant of all the circumstances involved.

The crew had acquitted themselves nobly. No fault was to be found with their being so dog-tired. In the past three weeks they had been on duty day after day, without an evening ashore. In the past three days and nights the going had been really hard.

Following their first fight they had the work of readying the ship for sea after their return from all-night Action Stations. Three times during the next night they had been called out to man their stations for at least an hour each time. During the day they had done the normal work of the ship and then gone to sea again, to man their Action Stations through another night.

Before the dawn came they had lost the *Athabaskan* and had fought furiously to win through themselves. Twice within forty-eight hours they had engaged and defeated the enemy. Victors, they felt they had earned a night in harbour. Instead they were being asked to work on past what seemed to be the limits of human endurance.

There was no grumbling. They were long past that stage. They came to their heavy task with the dumb acquiescence of exhaustion. Battered and hammered by battle, their tortured nerves were denied the opiate they sought in sleep and they moved shuffling, like automatons.

It seemed that only a miracle could bring a spark of life to these dull eyes and ease the intolerable burden of weariness that sagged their shoulders, but the miracle was there. They found they were not alone. They had good friends.

Huron's company had watched the weary Tribal come home from battle and comprehended their circumstances with understanding minds. This was more than just a ship in the same flotilla. This was their sister ship from Canada.

They didn't send signals of condolences or ask questions. They just got busy. Shore leave for afternoon and evening had been scheduled for *Huron* this day, probably the last shore leave they would have in a long time, but when the call came for volunteers every man on board stepped forward.

Two officers and fifty men went over to *Haida*. They didn't ask anyone's permission. The ammunition barge was alongside and, both ships being identical, they knew exactly where the ammunition had to be stored. Rolling up their sleeves they went to work.

When *Haida's* weary crew came shuffling aft after dinner to tackle the reammunitioning they stared with momentarily uncomprehending eyes before it dawned on them what was happening. They were told firmly what they could do, and not a single man was permitted to lift his hand or help in any way. It was the first of many instances in which this fine sister Tribal showed her sterling worth.

Haida could have asked for help from shore but that is not the way of the navy. Each ship and her company must be prepared to stand alone in their trials and difficulties. *Huron* knew that no help would be asked. For their understanding hearts and the help which was given, unsought and unrequested, *Haida* was grateful in a way that went far beyond words.

Good news seldom comes alone. About three o'clock the dockyard inspectors who had been checking the action damage announced the ship could not be readied for sea that night. At least three more days would be required to put her in shape.

Shore leave was piped therefore as soon as the reammunitioning was completed, so that those who wished to do so could spend the night ashore.

Now shore leave, to destroyers on operations such as these, is a rare and valued privilege, but it was indicative of the utter exhaustion of *Haida's* crew that less than half a dozen men took advantage of it, and these only to find a bed.

The ship was still far from cleaned up. Destroyer men sleep so much in their clothes that they look forward to getting them off for a night in harbour, but with sheets and blankets yet to be replaced it meant they would have to sleep again "all standing".

The accommodation in which a destroyer crew sleeps could not by any stretch of imagination be called commodious. Upwards of two hundred men are berthed in space most would consider insufficient for a one-family cottage in the country, but the moment supper was over *Haida's* company, except for the unfortunate duty watch, turned in and slept, the deep troubled sleep of exhaustion.

CHAPTER X

Have landed survivors.

Both the lads who had been swept off *Haida's* scramble net
as she started to steam clear of the French coast had gone
under as the wash of the seas along the hull sucked them
down. They had turned over end on end in the maze of
churning water above the propellers but their lifejackets
brought them up and when they surfaced they were in the
wake of the ship. As she drew away they could see the big
white letters of her number on the stern.

By a minor miracle they had survived what to their shipmates had looked like certain death, and were alive and un-
hurt in chilly but oil-free water. Above them the stars still
shone in the paling night sky. Inshore the land loomed in
plain view. That was the enemy side. England and safety
were over a hundred miles away to the northward. At a loss
what to do, they decided to float for a bit until they got their
bearings.

Some distance astern of them another man watched *Haida*
go, a man with a badly-broken arm and a gashed face, the
Torpedo Gunner's Mate of the *Athabaskan*. He could have
made the *Haida*. Why he didn't shows the stuff that makes
a Navy.

Swimming away from the sinking *Athabaskan*, the T.G.M.
had met the coxswain in the water. True to their training
they discussed the situation and figured what might best be
done. If the survivors were grouped in liferafts together
they felt there might be a better chance of survival or of
rescue. A number of the men were clinging to bits of floating wreckage and were isolated from the others. They set
to work to get them grouped.

107

When *Haida* came back, they were busily engaged on this, supporting between them a young seaman whom they were bringing over to a raft. In the semi-dark they looked at each other, the same thought in their minds. Both knew they could reach the *Haida* on their own but they would have to abandon their burden.

As if sensing their thoughts the burned, half-conscious lad they were supporting muttered, "Don't leave me," through his clenched teeth.

That was that. Nodding encouragement to him they continued their slow progress towards a raft. By the time they reached it and found a place for their burden *Haida* was preparing to go. They brought others in, all they could see, and then, worn out, sought refuge themselves.

The coxswain found a hand-hold on one raft but there was no place for the T.G.M. He swam to another. It was full and so was the cork float he came to next. At the others it was the same grim story. Tiring fast, he swam slowly away. It didn't look as if this was his lucky night. With a last effort that drained the remainder of his strength he turned over on his back and floated.

Things were getting hazy. He didn't feel the cold chill of the Channel seas any more. A warm slumber seemed to be creeping over him. It was pleasant and he had nothing left with which to fight against it. Dimly, like a dream, he seemed to hear voices far back in his mind and a big shadowy thing seemed to be looming over him.

He felt himself being moved as strong hands held him under the arms and he was hauled clear of the water. Somebody was shouting close to his face but all he could hear was "Haida's boat."

"Good old Haida," he muttered. "I knew she would get us."

108

They laid him gently down by the shelter of the engine and, just as he realized he had been saved, consciousness left him.

The motorboat had been having a busy and exciting time. The coxswain and his crew had decided the best plan for them to follow would be to pick up the isolated survivors first, the men who had been unable to reach a raft. They had hauled four water-soaked shivering men from the drink when they saw *Haida* getting under way. With an idea of lining up her course so that they could follow later they swung round some quarter mile astern and checked her course by running in her wake. They had completed their check and were about to turn back towards the *Athabaskan* survivors when a voice from the water was heard by the bowman, a lad from Vancouver.

He stared unbelievingly at the dark water for a moment, imagining he had heard the voice of his chum come faintly across the water from the direction of the receding *Haida*. He knew of course it must be a hallucination, that his chum was safely at work on board the speeding ship.

But the voice sounded again and this time it was stronger, with a faint bored note in it that was unmistakable. "Hi! Vancouver," it called. "How about a hitch."

The astonished bowman strained his eyes forward and saw a darker blob on the water off the starboard bow. Singing out to the coxswain, he conned the boat over and there, grinning up at him, was his chum from *Haida*.

It was a vigorous ghost. "Give me a hand up," it ordered. "This water's far too cold for swimming yet."

It was one of the two lads who had been swept off the scramble net. Feeling cold he had decided to swim for a bit and had sighted the motorboat. Once aboard he quickly directed them to the other lad who was still floating a couple

109

of hundred yards ahead. Both were in good shape and, apart from the cold and their wet clothes, had suffered no discomfort.

Good luck, which seemed to be with them up to that point, deserted them now. The engine spluttered and stopped and all their efforts to restart it proved unavailing. As helpless now as those they sought to save, they drifted with the wind and tide. Yet the Providence that watches over the brave was still amid the dark waters. Over on the port side they discerned the dark blob of another floating figure and, ripping up floorboards for paddles, they manoeuvred the heavy motorboat slowly towards it. In over the side they hauled another far-spent survivor, a signalman from *Athabaskan*.

It was heavy work handling the improvised paddles and all of them were tired. They were about to give up when the bowman sighted another floating figure. They yelled at him to swim over but the man in the water paid no attention. He was floating on his back. At first they thought he might be dead and then they saw one of his arms move feebly.

They paddled over and came alongside him. "It's the T.G.M.," ejaculated the bowman. "Look at his poor bloody face."

They lifted him carefully and brought him inboard. "What ship?" he muttered through blue lips. "It's the Haida's boat," they told him. It didn't seem to register at first and they laid him down by the engine where he would be sheltered and warm. One of them stripped off his outer jumper and wrapped it round the T.G.M. The strong gashed face relaxed a trifle. "Good old Haida," he muttered and then went out like a light.

The dawn was coming up fast. As they sat helplessly in

the boat while the stoker worked at the engine they looked towards the land. The German destroyer was still burning furiously on the beach and, as they looked at the salvo-smashed wreck, there came a sudden flash and then a great boom as it was rent by a violent explosion. The flames had obviously reached a magazine and burning debris and chunks of the hull were thrown high into the air.

In the boat the crew and the survivors who could stand got up on their feet and cheered. They knew that one was finished beyond redemption now.

Meanwhile precious minutes were slipping away. Well to the eastward they could see the black clusters of the *Athabaskan* survivors on the rafts. It was full daylight now and the sun, giving promise of a fine day ahead, was also making, moment by moment, their presence in these enemy waters increasingly dangerous. They wondered if they could get the engine started in time to rescue some of the men on the rafts before the enemy spotted them. They did their best to encourage the stoker but he was having a difficult time.

The intake was clogged and the stoker was unfamiliar with this type of Diesel engine. Before the war he had handled the engines of speedboats on Lake Muskoka but this one was resisting his best efforts.

Time was passing fast now and those who were not helping the stoker watched the sky and the land. The wounded T.G.M. still lay unconscious.

"Something's coming up round that headland," said the coxswain and they all looked over where he pointed.

It was ships all right, three of them in line ahead, not more than four miles away.

"Minesweepers!" observed the bowman. "I'd know 'em anywhere," he added ruefully, "I've seen enough of them."

111

Steaming directly towards the first group of survivors some three miles east the German minesweepers stopped there. Two seemed to be going closer to pick them up and then, with sinking hearts they saw the third minesweeper get under way again and steam directly towards them.

It looked bad, very bad. Those clustered in the after cockpit of the motorboat looked at each other and then one slowly took his knife off his belt and tossed it overboard. His pocket case, with his identification card, weighted with coins to make it sink, followed the knife. The others methodically followed his example. A knife was a weapon and prisoners found with weapons were liable to be shot. They had no desire to give the Krauts any excuses, for they were well aware how cheaply the enemy held life and what little excuse might be sufficient for them.

The stoker straightened up and wiped his eyes with his forearm. The enemy sweeper was barely a mile away now and seemed to be coming up fast. He looked at it grimly and gave the engine a disgusted glance. Bending down again he lifted a hammer and studied it for a moment, and then, in a last frantic effort which indicated it was all or nothing, he smashed the hammer down on the intake and pressed the starter button at the same time.

It caught. Coughing and spluttering, the engine started, while the men held their breath and waited, wondering if it would splutter and die again.

"Give me a hand somebody," yelled the stoker. "Hold this ruddy plug in place." Half a dozen willing hands reached to help him as the engine steadied reassuringly, the sweetest music any one of them had ever heard, and the motorboat surged ahead.

Sitting on the engine, the stoker coaxed her with words and hands and the coxswain, sitting on the tiller, headed the

112

boat straight into the choppy Channel seas, directly away from the rapidly approaching enemy.

Their first quick elation was only momentary. All out the motorboat was reputed to be able to do ten knots but they were not getting her full speed. As they watched tensely it became obvious that the German ship was slowly but steadily overhauling them. Their hearts sank as they watched her coming nearer.

The original lead of two thousand yards had been reduced to almost half that distance now. Tense and expectant, they waited to hear a shot come whistling over their heads or the rattle of machine guns sweeping the sea.

Then came the miracle. With the motorboat within easy reach and her little company ready to stop at the first command, the enemy minesweeper suddenly altered course, turned about and headed back toward her two consorts.

What prompted her they did not know. It could be that they were heading into a minefield or it might be that the German Captain figured they couldn't get away anyway and were foolish to try.

Whatever it was they thanked Providence and kept on going. Figuring that if they angled off the land, making plenty of westing and holding that course as long as they were in sight of the coast, they could then turn to seaward, they decided their course. This, they felt, would confuse any later pursuit.

It was a good plan if it had worked but seven miles off-shore the engine spluttered and died again, leaving them drifting once more.

They were in better condition than they had been to start with. The sun and wind were drying their clothes. Their cigarettes had been soaked but they spread them out to dry on the engine cover now. Someone produced a pipe and

113

when the tobacco was ready they filled it up and puffed Indian fashion, passing the pipe from one to another. After the smoke the stoker and two assistants went back to work on the engine.

"How's the time?" asked the stoker.

The coxswain consulted his wrist watch and answered that he figured it was about nine o'clock. The stoker turned back to work and then stopped, his head poised listening

The others heard it too. Faint and distant, it was the sound of aircraft and it was coming from seaward.

They could see them now, two fighters flying low above the waves and heading their way. They stood up waving and shouting. There was a Verey pistol in the boat and the coxswain fired it, the red flare showing plainly in the sky. Altering course, the two planes thundered towards them.

Sweeping in, about twelve feet above the surface and a hundred yards off, they went past, one on each side. The men in the boat could see the helmetted heads of the pilots looking at them as they waved happily at the planes.

An A.B., whose hobby was aircraft, stopped waving suddenly and, with a yell of "Krauts!" ducked down by the bulwarks. On wings and fuselages the markings were plain. They were Messerschmitts, 109's.

Their faces grim, the seamen watched them go. At first they thought the planes would circle back and machine-gun them but the fighters made directly in over the land. They knew now however that they would be reported to the enemy shore. No one said anything but they all turned impulsively towards the engine and tried to lend a hand.

The stoker had done a good job however and this time when he pressed the starter he did not have to use the hammer technique. The engine started. It was a bit ragged and far from its best but it was working and the motorboat started to forge slowly ahead once more.

Again they heard the buzz of planes but this time it was high and distant, a flight of bombers. They knew it would be the R.A.F. and they tried to attract their attention as they watched them go in towards the land, heading towards the smouldering destroyer. Bomb flashes and ack-ack fire were visible now and then the planes apparently went on for they lost sight of them.

All hands contributed their food supplies as the boat putted steadily seaward. Nearly every man had an emergency ration tin, containing malted milk tablets, barley sugar candy and chewing gum. The water had seeped into these but the malted milk tablets were still edible, so they dried them out and had half of one apiece.

The problem of what course to steer was the next point to come up for discussion for no one of them knew just where they had been operating on the French coast. One wanted to steer North-West; another thought North-East would be the proper course. After putting it to a vote they compromised and sailed due North.

They were tired and hungry. They needed food and medical supplies and the last was the worst. There was so little they could do for the unconscious T.G.M. beyond wrapping him in their clothes and trying to keep him warm. They were a long, long way from a friendly harbour yet they were hopeful and cheerful. *Haida* they knew would report them — as indeed she had. Planes had been searching for them but with no results, for a twenty-six foot motorboat is hard to find in hundreds of square miles of choppy seas. Of this they were not aware yet, and buoyed by strong hopes of a speedy rescue they held their slow course northwards towards the distant shores of England.

115

That night at seven o'clock a weary officer of *Haida,* still in his battle-dress after a long, hard day's work, fell asleep in the chart room while waiting for a phone call. He was aroused by the rumble of gunfire close at hand. Dazed, he glanced at his watch. The hands read twenty minutes to four. For a horrified moment he thought he must have dreamed that the ship had returned safely to harbour and that the battle must still be on. Stumbling out on deck he was reassured by the dim loom of the dock buildings. He saw the searchlights reaching their long fingers of light up into the skies and pin-pointing an enemy plane.

From ships and shore batteries a tremendous barrage was going up. Several fires were burning ashore, well up in the port away from the docks. The planes were obviously re-tiring now and were getting out of range. On the bridge a dim figure lifted a microphone and ordered the pom-pom to belay firing. Down the ladder came the Captain, his face drawn and tired, and went aft to his cabin.

It was Sunday morning, April the thirtieth, 1944. The officer's first impulse was to go back to sleep in view of the hour. He tried but couldn't get off again. Hunting up a cup of coffee he took it into the Signal Distribution Office, under the bridge, known as the S.D.O.

He had just taken a sip when the telephone rang. It was the shore line. Automatically reaching for a pencil and signal pad, he lifted the receiver.

Incredulity and then a glad amazement filled his eyes as he heard the operator at the other end.

"Repeat please, repeat," he requested.

"The West Cornwall Hospital . . . yes. Sighted by R.A.F. planes twenty miles south of the Lizard . . . yes. Picked up and brought into Penzance by Air-Sea rescue launch . . . yes.

116

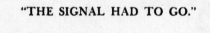

"THE SIGNAL HAD TO GO."

Six survivors from H.M.C.S. Athabaskan and five from H.M.C.S. Haida, all ratings.

"Repeat that please. Have you any further details?

"Six survivors from Athabaskan . . . yes. Three boat's crew and two survivors from Haida . . . yes, that's right. These two are survivors from Haida. They were lost from the scramble net. The motorboat has been brought in to Falmouth . . . right? Good. Will you let me have the names now please."

The message finished he reached for the phone marked C.O., and then hesitated. The Captain had been practically without sleep for three days and nights and now this was his first chance to get caught up. He got a great deal less sleep than anyone else on board and he had been turned out once already tonight.

The signal of course would have to be forwarded to the Chief of Naval Staff in Ottawa right away. There were homes in Canada where this news would bring swift relief to anxious hearts. He could send it on, but somehow he felt the Captain would want to know now.

Leaving the office and making his way aft he looked into the Captain's cabin and essayed a quiet "Sir!"

The Captain was in his bunk, lying awake. He turned his head to look up at the doorway and then switched on the light by the bunk.

"Yes," he said quietly, "what is it?"

There was a world of weariness in his voice but as he heard the news the grim lines of fatigue etched deep in his tired face relaxed and his eyes lightened.

"Good," he said. "Make arrangements to go down there later in the day. See how they are and find out what happened. They may have news for us of the others. You

117

may be able to bring them back. They must be looked after."

The West Cornwall Hospital, when two officers finally reached it that evening, was a quiet oasis in the thoroughly blacked-out Cornish seaport. The Matron, one of these fine women who have devoted their lives to the nursing profession, took them at once to the ward where the survivors were housed.

"It's been difficult to keep them in bed," she told them. "We've had a great many survivors here since the war started but never any quite as cheerful as this crowd. They wanted to get up this morning and leave right after breakfast."

"They really do seem to be in splendid shape though and by tomorrow the doctor thinks it will be all right for them to leave. The one with the broken arm, its really broken badly in two places, will have to stay with us for a few weeks yet, but the others are all right. They're wonderful lads."

When the visitors entered the ward the patients, despite the late hour, were far from sleep. As soon as they saw who was arriving there were delighted smiles and four or five of them jumped out of bed and crowded around, all talking at once and eager to relate their experiences.

The motor had failed again around noon but they had persevered and got it going. This time it ran steadily. The sun warmed them and apart from the lack of food they didn't feel too bad.

About half-past six in the evening they saw two planes coming from the direction of France. Believing they were the German fighters coming back, they ducked for cover beneath the boat housing and it was not until they were almost overhead that they spotted the R.A.F. markings. They went a bit crazy then, waving and signalling "Canada" to the Spitfires.

They were spotted all right. The two fighters stayed above them for an hour and then were relieved by two more fighters and a Lancaster bomber. About ten o'clock one of the fighters came in close and circled. Then they saw a ship coming. It was an Air-Sea rescue launch.

Taken aboard, they were wrapped in blankets and then fed by the launch crew. After a meal washed down by a noggin of hot rum they felt much better and were sped into Penzance. The motorboat was picked up later and taken in tow by a Fairmile of the Coastal Patrol which brought it into Falmouth.

It was quite a story they had to tell and it was three in the morning before the last account had been taken from the *Athabaskan's* T.G.M. That able man, in careful, measured words described what had happened and then relaxed with a slow smile. He had done his duty.

Leaving the quiet hushed hospital, the officers sought quarters for the night elsewhere, much to the disappointment of the Matron. That good lady, as they had reason to suspect, was of the opinion that they should be hospitalized also and they respected her ability too much to take any chances. Exhaustion was dogging their footsteps but they knew how hard it can be to get out of hospital once inside.

Next morning the doctor concluded his inspection and approved departure for everyone but the T.G.M. It was the only possible decision and though he felt a bit lonely, he bore up well. He was in good hands and would receive excellent care and attention.

The next stop was at the local naval depot. Here new uniforms were issued to those who required them and they were "kitted up", as the replacement of missing items in a seaman's kit is termed. That completed, they were issued with travelling warrants to Plymouth.

119

Arriving there the *Athabaskan* survivors went to barracks and *Haida's* men returned to their ship. Their first welcome was from Bunker. That able seaman had been proceeding up town on liberty, heading for a pub in the vicinity of the station, where the bartender had a dog's understanding, when he caught sight of them. Bunker immediately abandoned his own plans in order to give them a vociferous welcome and trotted proudly back with them to the ship.

They felt glad to be back in the familiar surroundings of their floating home and the pride their shipmates took in them was a reward more than ample for what they had come through. They had to sit down, have their every need attended to and tell the story over and over again to their admiring messmates. Finally, to avert attention they turned the conversation to Bunker, telling how he had found and welcomed them at the station.

Bunker was building quite a reputation since his first engagement. Since his early puppyhood he had refused to eat his meals off the deck. Taking his place on a bench in the seamen's mess, he sat up at a table and ate off a plate like every other Jack. His "mick" had to be slung every night in harbour too.

"You should have seen him at Liberty Men tonight," remarked Red. "The Officer of the Day inspected every liberty man in the lineup and passed up Bunker.

"He growled blue murder but the officer pretended not to notice him. Finally Bunker walks over and gave him a yank in the bottom of his pants with his teeth and looks up at him as much as to say, 'What the heck!'

" 'Get back in line,' shouts the officer and Bunker slinks back to the end of the line and faces front. He checked him over then, feeling his collar and looking behind his ears. 'O.K.,' he says and Bunker marches ashore with the gang."

"He sure got corned last night," remarked the Leading Hand.

"Aw he was just celebrating," said Red.

"Celebrating!" returned the Killick, "I'll say he was. All the mateys in the dockyard heard about him. He was as drunk as a skunk, fighting half the dogs in town and chasing the bitches up and down back alleys half the night."

"It's these bartenders," said Red. "He likes a sip of beer and they know it but they let every slap-happy Jack who wants to buy him a drink spike his beer with gin and whisky."

"Boy you shoulda seen him trying to turn in last night. He climbed up on the locker an' tried to get into his mick," put in Joe. "I couldn't sleep an' I was lying watching him. He gits his forepaws on the mick, steadies it an' then gives a lurch an' tries to get aboard. Every time he falls right over an' lands on the deck.

"Finally he gives up an' curls up on the locker. The Duty Officer finds him when he's making rounds. 'Get in your mick Able Seaman Bunker,' he says, 'or I'll put you on report.' Bunker looks at him an' tries again. If the D.O. hadn't been so tired he'd have died laughing. He picks Bunker up by the scruff of the neck an' puts him in. Bunker's grateful so he reaches up an' licks the D.O.'s face with his beery whiskers.

" 'You're a drunken old rascal,' says the D.O., 'an' if you don't watch your step you'll be in the rattle!' Bunker grunts happy and sounds off with a real snore. What a dog!"

"Bunker's O.K., ain't you Bunker," said the returned bowman from the motorboat as he rubbed the whiskered ruffian's head.

121

"Sure he's O.K." added the other returnees as they rose to strip off and hit the hay. They were tired, all of them, and by ten o'clock the only sound in the messdecks was the rhythmic breathing of soundly-sleeping men with Bunker, sober tonight, curled happily in their midst.

Gran Macdonald
RCNVR 45

"DRINKS WERE THE ORDER OF THE DAY."

CHAPTER XI

Destroyers will carry out coastal bombardment as directed to cover large-scale amphibious landing exercises in designated area.

Repairs, which were quite extensive, could not be completed under several days, it was found, and *Haida's* company, as a consequence, enjoyed the luxury of nightly shore leave and opportunities to look around this part of England. Ashore they found the fame of their exploits had got around and they were given a warm welcome.

Free drinks were the order of the day in more than one local hostelry to which they extended their patronage and quite a few of the lads made friends and were invited to quiet firesides where they could stretch their legs and feel at home.

Haida however was getting ready for sea again. With a new seaboat, new liferafts and sundry other gear which her officers had taken the opportunity to install she was in good shape now for a new phase of operations, a phase associated with what would come to be known as the greatest amphibious operation in history.

The short spell in harbour which was now drawing to a close had already done the ship's company a world of good. The regular hours of sleep and daily exercise in the sunshine for which this part of England is famous had accomplished a great deal. Already the tortured memories of the last grim fight were losing their sharpness. They would never be forgotten but new duties and their attendant new interests were rousing them and centering their thoughts on the great tasks which lay ahead.

Saturday morning dawned clear and fine, bringing considerable speculation on board as to whether the ship would be lucky enough to stay in port over the weekend. When lunchtime came with no intimation of any impending change a number of officers and men went ashore on short afternoon liberty to see what they could scull up in the way of interest.

Up at the Plymouth dog-racing track a big and cosmopolitan crowd had gathered, filling the stands and the paddock to watch the sport of the "little fellow" and back their fancy at the "totes". The blue of the seaforces was in the majority but soldiers of the United States, red-beretted British paratroops, Wrens, Waafs, A.T.S. girls, nurses, shipyard and munition workers combined to give colour and life to the animated scene.

Plymouth, being an invasion port and well inside the invasion area, had been closed off and guarded from the rest of the country for some weeks now in preparation for the great D day that loomed ahead. Whether it was a week or a month away no one knew or cared to hazard a guess but all felt in their hearts the omnipresence of its impending arrival.

Today however it was springtime, even in warworn England. Tomorrow the greatest armada in history might sail forth to triumph or disaster but today still belonged to the laughing, talking crowds who were putting the sombre thoughts of the morrow determinedly aside.

At three o'clock the races started and all interest was focussed on the greyhounds. Whoops, cheers and groans urged the straining dogs as they pursued the rabbit on the rail round the mile track and hundreds of pounds flowed through the tote wickets as excitement gripped the speculators.

Then, at ten minutes to four, when the dogs were being

124

paraded for the next race an announcement came over the loudspeaker system which brought a sudden hush among the crowds.

"Ladies and gentlemen," said the announcer, "we must interrupt our race schedule at this time to make a most important announcement on behalf of the naval authorities. A general recall signal has been made by all cruisers and destroyers in port and all officers and men are required to return to their ships immediately."

Faces were thoughtful, and there were many mute questions in the eyes of the listeners as hundreds of naval personnel began to filter quietly through the crowds towards the gate, among them four young Tribal officers with Canada badges on their shoulders.

"I guess we had that lot," remarked the "Chief" philosophically.

"Another race and we would have cleaned up. Our system was just coming due for a dividend," said the "Gunner" regretfully. "Wonder what's up?"

Outside the dog track they caught a bus and headed for the dockyard. The recall notices were being prominently displayed in front of every pub, and police prowl cars, fitted with loudspeakers, were also announcing the recall as they cruised the streets.

"Maybe the Germans are trying to invade us first," said a Lieutenant thoughtfully, "must be something big or they wouldn't recall the whole harbour."

"Uh uh!" ejaculated a sophisticated member of the party, "it's Saturday afternoon and the Admiral's going to play tennis. He's just heard the 10th D.F.'s in port and he's decided all striking forces are a bad influence. No drunks or fights in town tonight. The soldiers can drink all the beer and flannel onto the gals."

125

With this version all four solemnly agreed although they listened with interest to the speculation in the wardroom when they got back aboard.

"Maybe it's the invasion," said a brash young officer brightly and then subsided suddenly as he realized the amused contempt aroused by his suggestion.

"Tell him somebody," said a lounging senior, "or is he too young to know?"

"What's the use?" another asked, "he wouldn't understand anyway."

"Oh, is he from Toronto?" rejoined the first speaker sweetly.

At that about half the wardroom, to whom that much-abused city was home, piled on the speaker simultaneously and he disappeared beneath a mass of struggling bodies, arms and legs.

Getting to his feet, the junior, cause of it all, looked around aggrievedly and remarked, with some dudgeon, that it was only a suggestion anyway. "We are supposed to have an invasion sometime aren't we?" he concluded.

"You tell me when," returned the Surgeon belligerently. "There'll be no invasion this year. All that stuff is just talk." His tone however lacked conviction and it was evident he was thinking of casualties.

Two officers there, already familiar with the invasion plans and dates, listened quietly and made no comment. Even to them it still seemed a far-away possibility and they had learned that Admiralty is quite capable when necessary of deep-dyed plans of its own. They were, of course, sworn to secrecy and not even to their shipmates could they divulge a word of what they knew.

When the ship finally sailed, however, in the small hours of the morning, the word got around of what was under

126

way. They were bound on a full-dress rehearsal of a beach-head invasion, selected for its similarity to another coast across the Channel.

All hands were keenly interested. There had been so much speculation about the invasion, so much discussion and so many suggested plans published that they anticipated something really spectacular.

The loom of the false dawn was over the land as they closed the appointed area to commence the preliminary bombardment. To seaward a great invasion fleet, which had arrived off the rendezvous during the night, was steaming into position, screened by cruisers and other destroyers.

The air barrage, which had been listed as the prelude to the bombardment, had been cancelled because of weather or some other complications. It was a cold, misty morning and the beach, with a ravine and low hills behind it, looked natural and deserted.

Opening fire against the sites of the plotted fixed shore defences the destroyers went into action first and were followed by the heavier guns of the cruisers. Bursts of sand and dirt could be seen thrown up as shells landed on the beach and then, as the range lifted, in the ravine and on the low hills beyond. The shallows were given a heavy strafing by the cruisers to destroy underwater obstacles.

Infantry landing ships had cleared their landing craft and these were now approaching the line from which they would make their dash for the beach.

The destroyers moved inshore now, firing steadily and, as the signal came to lift the barrage, the landing craft started their run for the beach. It looked like a standard operation of the type used in earlier landings. While aircraft would be present on the big show the seamen were not particularly impressed.

There were however a few tricks that had not been played and now they saw one of them come into action. They had noticed several long, flat, bargelike ships hovering astern of the landing craft. As the run for the beach started these followed and then, with a suddenness that came as a complete surprise to the watchers, they showed their purpose.

The noise of muffled explosions came across the water, followed by swishing sounds and from the foresections of these strange craft came an eruption of rocket bombs. The first flight was hardly in the air before it was followed by another and then still more in quick succession.

What the rocket flights did to that beach was almost unbelievable. On the shore and for hundreds of yards above it, not a single square yard escaped the awful avalanche of death that was showered upon it. The ground reverberated with the shock of the missiles until it seemed impossible that even an insect could survive in that area, so intense was the bombardment.

As the amazed watchers looked at the clouds of dust and smoke settling back, the first of the landing craft touched the beach. Down went the ramps and the troops debouched ashore. Almost as swiftly the first of the tanks and armoured vehicles followed on their heels.

Late in the day, when it was all over, the destroyers returned to harbour, their crews convinced that invasion was not only imminent but eminently practical with weapons such as these. This was close-quarters fighting surpassing their highest expectations. For the first time the invasion took on the aspects of reality in their minds.

Shore leave now became virtually a thing of the past and the Tribals were kept busy. Many nights found them back on their old beat off the French Coast, either on covering operations or looking for trouble. Each morning, however,

"INVASION WAS IMMINENT AND PRACTICAL."

on their return to port, they would note fresh preparations for the great Day.

Plymouth harbour was becoming increasingly reminiscent of Halifax. Fleets of the sturdy little minesweepers which they had so often watched sweeping the approaches to that great strategic convoy seaport of the North Atlantic had come over to Britain and were based here to work in Channel waters. They would be the advance elements of the invasion armadas, sweeping clear seaways into the French Coast. Often on entering or leaving harbour the Tribals would pass them. On these occasions their men always stood a little straighter and were quick to return the pipe of those sturdy little Canadian-built and -manned ships. The men of the 10th D.F., being members of the striking forces, rated as the aristocrats of the ships based in the Western Approaches Command, but they took their caps off to the sweepers. They knew their worth.

Also arriving now were some of the famous North Atlantic escort groups. River Class destroyers like *Restigouche, St. Laurent, Skeena, Chaudière* and *Qu'Appelle* steamed in and with them came many of the new frigates and corvettes to deal with the U-boats which Admiralty anticipated in the Channel once invasion operations got under way. All these Canadians made the harbour seem like a little bit of Canada. It was just like being at home.

The big base was filling up slowly. More than one leviathan of the Royal Navy had arrived and the United States was being increasingly represented with a large and varied fleet. On the U.S.S. Augusta, the trim cruiser which had carried President Roosevelt on several occasions, the Stars and Stripes of "Old Glory" flew proudly, as it did on lean destroyers, torpedo boats, landing ships and craft of many types. It seemed fitting that here, where the Mayflower had sailed with the Pilgrim Fathers, the New World should be strongly represented.

Four more destroyers, the Polish ships *Blyskawica* and *Piorun,* and H.M.S. Eskimo and H.M.S. Javelin, had arrived to reinforce the 10th D.F., bringing it up to eight heavy-hitting ships. The light cruisers *Black Prince* and *Bellona* were temporarily withdrawn now as they would have another part to play.

A few nights later the Poles showed their mettle when they sailed with *Tartar, Ashanti, Haida* and *Huron* on an offensive patrol. Steaming along the English coast, the powerful force arrived off Land's End at dusk and turned seaward.

A plane came out from over the land, flying low. Most of the ships presumed it friendly but the Poles opened fire. They were quite right. It was a German reconnaissance plane, as a hurried check quickly revealed.

Later it was learned that one of the ships had managed to tune in on the pilot's wavelength and had heard him singing gustily in German as he flew up and down their line.

There were no operations off the French Coast that night. The Force had been spotted and as a result every light would be turned off and every enemy ship ordered inshore to shelter. The alertness of the Polish destroyer however had made a favourable impression on all hands.

The Poles indeed gave every evidence of being worthy allies. Each of their ships carried a British signal officer and signal detachment of a Yeoman and other rates so that they could work in company with British ships with the minimum of inconvenience due to language barriers.

In harbour the Poles became frequent visitors on board the Tribals. They were pleasant companions and loved to sing. On one memorable occasion they insisted on singing one of their favourite songs under the proper conditions. The particular conditions required were to turn out the lights in *Haida's* wardroom, roll back the carpet and then light a bonfire with newspapers on the steel deck. Sitting cross-legged around this they sang their song, a haunting gypsy melody. When it was over they put out the little fire and did a kind of Conga dance, led by their First Lieutenant. They were cheerful blokes.

Blyskawica had a mascot, a pet monkey which was a constant source of amusement to *Haida's* and *Huron's* men when *Blyskawica* berthed alongside them. One afternoon the Captain sent his steward over to the Polish ship. A naval reservist, the steward was a short, stocky man, with all the dignity of a short man added to that of his position.

Crossing the gangplank, he walked up the maindeck of the Polish ship and, stopping by the Officer of the Day, he passed his message. The monkey, lying in wait with his long leash coiled beside him, dashed out and nimbly swarmed up the steward's trousers. After worrying him a moment in the nether regions he dropped off and retreated to his hideout.

Completely ignoring this ignominious attack, the steward walked back in a dignified manner to his own ship. The Surgeon, who had been standing on the quarterdeck with the Torpedo Officer, laughing heartily at the monkey's assault on the steward's dignity, suddenly noticed spots on the deck dropping from the steward's trousers.

"Where's the blood coming from?" he asked.

Unaware that he had been bitten, the steward felt his back end and then looked at his reddened hand. Whisked into Sick Bay, and his pants taken off, he was found to have taken quite a gash from the monkey's sharp teeth. The

131

wound had to be treated immediately for poison but the
steward was more concerned about his trousers. From then
on the nimble monk was his pet aversion.

It was a good thing that in these last days of tense waiting and watching before the great event, the men found
ways and means of relaxing.

The never-ending good-natured rivalry between Navy
and Air Force provided a spicy moment towards the end of
May when there were many naval chuckles at the expense
of their airborne comrades.

Haida, Huron and *Ashanti,* patrolling to seaward off the
English coast one evening, heard the engines of a plane
approaching. He was flying low and outlined against the
starlit sky they recognized his silhouette as friendly. To
their amazement however he didn't act friendly.

Coming in on them he made what seemed like a bombing run above the ships and then came back and did it
again. As he turned for another one the Bridge Watch
wondered what he was up to and the Captain reminded
them to "keep your knees bent".

The Officer of the Watch, annoyed by this movement of
the plane and knowing he must have been advised of their
position and patrol, looked up and snapped, "Why doesn't
that fellow stay where he belongs. He's nine miles to eastward of his eastern position limit."

The plane disappeared to the westward then but shortly
afterwards a message was received from the land, advising
them that aerial reconnaissance had revealed the presence
of three E Boats on a similar course nine miles ahead.
Engines revved up and the destroyers swept off on search.
They had been looking for an E boat for a long time now
and this looked like a good chance.

With every lookout on the alert they combed the area

thoroughly, only to find, after considerable time had passed, that they were chasing themselves. The aerial navigator had been just nine miles out on his reckoning, nine miles to the eastward of where he should have been. His three E boats were three Tribal Class destroyers, more than three times as long and vastly bulkier than E boats.

The sailors laughed, long, low and heartily at their comrades of the air for that one and wondered next time they got an E boat report just what had been sighted. "Some night they'll see the Queen Elizabeth and report they've sighted an enemy destroyer," suggested the grinning Officer of the Watch. However, the Air Force was to have its turn before long.

CHAPTER XII

Being in all respects ready for war ships of the 10th D.F. will sail at 1400 and take up station for Operation Neptune.

Plymouth harbour, on the first day of June in the year of grace nineteen hundred and forty-four, presented an amazing spectacle and an impressive panorama of amphibious might. Ships of all shapes and sizes were everywhere, crowding the anchorages to such an extent that an overflow had to be accommodated outside in the shelter of Cawsand Bay.

Mingled with battleships, cruisers, destroyers, frigates, corvettes and minesweepers flying the White Ensign of the British Commonwealth, the Stars and Stripes of the United States, the flags of Free France, Poland and Norway among the smaller ships, was a big and motley fleet of infantry and tank landing ships, smaller landing craft, rocket gunships, tugs and all the floating paraphernalia of invasion on a mighty scale.

They were loading for the big event at last. All shore leave had been cancelled for both ship and base personnel, and a deep area of the south coast of England had been closed off by roadblocks and armed troops for weeks now as the forces gathered for the thrust that would take them southwards into France.

Silent seamen watched the long lines of tanks, self-propelled guns, jeeps, trucks, ducks, amtracks, ambulances and infantry filing into the multitude of ships in the bright June sunshine. This was but one of the invasion ports. They knew that all the way up the Channel shore and round into the great Port of London similar scenes were being enacted, in some areas on an even greater scale than here.

134

Grant Macdonald
RCNVR. 45

"SILENT SEAMEN WATCHED THE LONG LINE OF TANKS."

For the Tribals a role had been assigned which they received with mixed feelings. Their task would be a responsible one, engendered by necessity, but they would not participate in the bombardment of the French Coast. Although an important section of the naval forces of the invasion, they would not go inshore to cover the landings.

Strong German destroyer forces were known to be based on Brest and the Gironde. H.M. cruisers *Glasgow* and *Enterprise* had sunk three and damaged others late in December. In April *Haida* had disposed of two more but there were still enough to form a formidable force. That they would be grouped for an attack on the invasion lines was an inescapable conclusion. It would in all probability be a heavy attack, delivered with all the forces at their command. If they could break through the ships of the 10th D.F. and reach the invasion lines a serious situation might easily develop.

To the Tribals therefore was entrusted the task of guarding the Western Approaches, to meet and defeat any attack which the Germans might mount in these waters against the great armadas making for the French beachheads. In these now-familiar seas they would be carrying out their traditional role.

Sailing time that evening found them slipping moorings and proceeding through a hushed and crowded harbour. Lined up on deck the crews stood silent and observant as they passed between the long lines of landing craft, crowded with helmetted and camouflaged troops, and threaded their way through the maze of shipping to the seagate.

The soldiers looked bronzed and fit but they were very quiet. There was none of the usual quipping and waving as the grim fighting ships moved slowly seawards, advance guards of the great host that soon would follow. The

135

soldiers looked long and hard at the fighting ships' guns, as if realizing that it was upon these guns they would be dependent until they reached and landed on the shores of France. It was a solemn moment.

Outside, the Channel seas were choppy and, as the ships steamed swiftly southwards towards their patrol area those who knew the schedule were pessimistic of the invasion getting under way during this period. No landing craft could live for long in these turbulent waters and what a two-week postponement of the operation might involve they did not care to contemplate. Preparations had advanced too far to halt.

By morning, however, the weather had moderated a little. The seas still looked too rough for the smaller craft but weather reports were favourable and there was a good chance of improvement during the day. In the Tribals the unusual circumstance of being at sea in mid-channel waters in daylight was having a heartening effect.

Since the fall of France these waters had been conspicuously devoid of surface craft in the daylight hours. Too many land-based aircraft were conveniently located on either side or on patrol for the comfort of any unfortunate mariner in this vicinity. Only when night had cloaked the narrow waters in darkness did they venture forth.

Now, after a lapse of years, surface fighting-ships were coming out into the open again in these seas and it was like the loom of dawn breaking over better days. So effective were the pre-invasion Allied air patrols over the Channel on this day that there was little likelihood of any attack from enemy aircraft.

The long day passed without incident. The crew, in two watches, manned defence stations alternately, but nothing stirred on the lonely waters and it was not until the sun was

136

"A GUN CAPTAIN REASSURED THEM SWIFTLY."

slanting down to the evening skies that they heard the electrifying news. The invasion was on.

Over the ship's public address system the Captain announced that the signal had been received which meant that the invasion was under way. He outlined their own duty and its importance in the general operational scheme. When he had finished, copies of the personal message to each man from the Commander-in-Chief were distributed to the ship's company.

It was the big show at last. At this very moment many of the landing craft would be at sea and on their way to the rendezvous off the French beaches in the morning. The minesweepers were already at work, sweeping, buoying and lighting a clear channel leading right into the invasion beaches under the German guns.

The seas were still running quite high, with a nasty Channel chop that made the sailors feel sorry for the soldiers who would be in the smaller landing craft now. They were bound to be tossed around and be wretchedly seasick before they got across. And to have to land on a hostile shore in that condition would not be easy.

A gun captain, hearing his crew express their doubts on that subject, reassured them swiftly. "These pongos will be so glad to get ashore that nothing on God's green earth will stop them," he stated decisively. "And don't think they won't fight to stay there," he added; "anything would be better to them than going back. They've all got seasickness pills anyway, even if they don't know whether they're any good or not."

As they quested up the Channel on their patrol the Tribals got their first glimpse of one of the long, seemingly unending processions of ships making for the buoyed channel. It was an amazing and inspiring sight, a parade of the smaller

137

landing craft which had already been at sea for more than ten hours, chugging doggedly onwards. Steaming close in, they ran up the line and then sheered off to the South-West.

Between midnight and one o'clock they were patrolling to the westward of the Cherbourg peninsula. To the eastward the cross-channel traffic was like a scene from Piccadilly or Times Square at six o'clock on a busy peacetime evening, but here, to seaward of the fringes of the invasion, the seas were dark and silent under the stars.

It was a warm night. In *Haida,* with coats and mufflers loosened, every man was at his Action Station ready for trouble. It seemed impossible to believe that by this time the Germans would not be fully aware of what was impending and attack by E boat, U boat, destroyers, aircraft or some of Hitler's vaunted secret weapons was looked for at any moment.

They waited in silence for what seemed an unbearably long time, and then suddenly their straining ears heard from far off the faint drone of airplane engines. The drone became a rushing roar, and then a great thunder that filled the sky. Lookouts strained their eyes apprehensively upwards but the planes were coming from the British coast and were friendly.

"Here they come," said the Officer of the Watch, smiling happily in the darkness; "it's the big night all right. These fellows will be landing in France in another half hour."

A mighty armada of planes and gliders was coming over, flying just above the masts of the ships. Each showed a light underneath and they looked like a great swarm of fireflies in the summer night. There seemed to be no end to them. It was the American airborne division with more than a thousand planes.

The men on the destroyers looked up in silent admiration

138

and wished them a blessing. There was courage and high adventure up there, coursing through the skies to bring the dawn of liberation to the night-cloaked land of France. In their swift exultant passage could be sensed something of their magnificent spirit.

Over Guernsey a German searchlight snapped on, followed by others, all pointing upwards towards the heavens. High above the land could be seen the bursting flak of anti-aircraft guns now but the great formations of planes seemed to ignore it as they swept on in towards the dark mainland.

Something of the mounting excitement had communicated itself to the men in the ships and they eagerly discussed the chances of success for the paratroops' mission. There were no qualms as to whether the beach-heads could be successfully achieved or not. All hands felt that with these men from the skies softening up the defences inland the landings could not fail to back them up.

Dawn, breaking slowly and mistily over the Channel seas, found the Tribals some twenty miles off the French coast and still no sign of the enemy. There were many planes going over but they were all Allied, marked with the broad white bands of the aerial forces of liberation, just as the white star of the U.S. forces had been adopted as the identifying insignia of all Allied tanks, guns and vehicles, British, U.S., Canadian, French and Polish. News-hungry, the seamen eagerly scanned every signal and checked every broadcast. When word that the landings had been successful reached them they were tremendously elated.

Signalmen and communications ratings became, for the moment, the most popular men aboard. Men clustered around the S.D.O. eager for every scrap of gossip, and listened intently as news was passed over the ship's public address system. The Navigating Officer, taking a turn on the quarterdeck before going down for lunch, found himself beset by questioners.

He was in a particularly good mood. Like other seamen who had run the gauntlet of the Channel in the dark days of the war and taken part in the evacuation from France he had lived for the day of the return to the continent. Now that it had come he felt that a blot on British arms was being wiped out.

"Rommel's on the run," he told the questioners happily. "He's being squeezed right between these skybirds you saw last night and the troops going in on the beach-heads. The Yanks are right in there along with the rest of them and they're going to make old Rommel, Rundstedt and all these other rascals run for their lives."

The first jubilation, once they knew the beach-heads had been secured, began to give way to disappointment by the second day over their own seemingly inactive part. *Haida's* company wanted to get right in there on the beach-heads and take a crack at the Krauts too. It would be a poor show for them, they reflected, if they were listed as taking part in the greatest amphibious operation in history without seeing a single enemy or firing a single shot.

Officers and men took a dim view of inaction in history-making hours like these. Far far better than this would have been employment in coastal bombardment they figured. Because nothing had happened to make them think otherwise they nattered, after the habit of sailormen, of the High Command's lack of foresight in this seeming wastage of first-class fighting forces.

However, the turn of the Tribals to get into the thick of things was at hand and the wisdom of the High Command's disposal of its sea forces was soon to be apparent. It was on their own fighting record and gunpower that they had been given the honour of this position. Now they were to justify that choice.

Accurate aerial reconnaissance had revealed the intelligence that two Narvik class destroyers had left the Gironde, presumably for Brest to rendezvous with other German destroyer forces there. Some German surface operation was evidently under contemplation.

In the Tribals the chance of an encounter with the German Roeder class ships, as the improved Narviks were called, had been a subject of interested speculation. According to available intelligence, which was somewhat sketchy in this respect, these ships were over four hundred and seventy feet long and mounted five-point-nine inch guns. They were also reputed to be faster than the Tribals.

The German Elbing Class destroyers, to which the enemy ships destroyed at Sept Iles and Ile de Vierge by the Tribals in April belonged, had put up a good fight. Every seaman who had fought in these actions had learned to respect them. They were no push-overs. What then of the much bigger and more heavily gunned Narviks? It looked as if the odds might be against the Tribals should this encounter develop.

The 10th D.F. had been brought to its full strength of eight ships and now, refuelled and ready in all respects for war, mounted guard in the Western Approaches. Strategists had decided the flotilla could operate best in two divisions. In the first division, which took up its patrol position closest to the French Coast, were H.M.S. Tartar, H.M.S. Ashanti, H.M.C.S. Haida, and H.M.C.S. Huron, in that order. In the second division, which would patrol farther to seaward, but in close touch, were the Polish destroyers *Blyskawica* and *Piorun,* with the British H.M.S. Eskimo and H.M.S. Javelin.

Overcast, with low clouds and rainsqualls, brought promise of dirty weather ahead on this evening of June the eighth as

141

the flotilla steamed to the westward through its patrol area, restlessly seeking signs of the enemy.

Hands had gone to Action Stations at half-past ten. Now, about one o'clock in the morning, with nothing happening, they had almost resigned themselves to a quiet night. Down in the flats the ammunition supply parties, fully dressed and equipped, were stretched out on the steel decks beside the magazine hatches, resting as they waited what the night might bring forth.

Time was dragging tediously on the bridge also when a message was received which brought swift alertness. It was a report from *Tartar,* the leading destroyer. She had contacted suspicious echoes up ahead.

As their own instruments probed and swept the dark seas to the westward the bridge crews waited, tense and expectant. The Gunnery Officer, as soon as the first signal had been received, barked two words into the telephone which spread swiftly throughout the ship.

CHAPTER XIII

Four destroyers bearing 240, *three miles, their course unknown.*

"Stand by!" called the Gunnery Officer into his telephone.

Down in the flats the resting men came to their feet with a rush and took their positions in the lines. Shells were ready to their hands. Sufficient ammunition was already up for the guns to open fire on but if action developed a constant flow would have to be maintained to feed the hungry muzzles. They stood ready as the ships of the division deployed for action.

By this time *Haida's* own searching instruments had found and ranged the echoes. There were four, enemy destroyers. Ranges and bearings were passed immediately to the transmitting station, far below. Automatically calculated there and passed to the gun turrets, they set these in motion, the long barrels swinging round and elevating as they were ranged on the targets.

"Open fire when ready!" commanded the Captain.

A burst of gunfire broke out up ahead as the leading destroyer opened fire and spread down the line as others followed. They were racing at high speed now, the whine of the turbines adding its eerie note to the other noises.

Starshell bursting over the reported bearing revealed the enemy ships. Taken by surprise, they were making a hasty attempt to go around and make to Westward. The two rear ships succeeded in doing so but the speeding Tribals, crashing headlong into the enemy formation with all their guns blazing, made it impossible for the two leading German ships to go about, and their line was pierced.

General action was joined as the ships engaged. The range

143

had closed so swiftly that the Tribals were shooting on at least one target at point blank range and the Germans were shooting back desperately.

It was a fierce and bitter melee there in the shell-torn darkness as both sides threw the full weight of their armament at each other. The scream of shells and the crescendo of fire reached a wild intensity as they fought it out.

Maintaining the advantage of the initial onslaught the grim Tribals gave the enemy ships no chance to recover. One, slashed repeatedly by their salvos, staggered off into the darkness and another went off in a tangent northward while the two which had turned about fled to the westward making smoke.

The range had been too close for the Tribals to escape unscathed and now from *Tartar* came a brief: "I am on fire." Hit by several salvos through her bridge superstructure at point-blank range as she led the division crashing into the enemy line, the gallant British destroyer had taken punishment.

Haida and *Huron,* racing up behind *Ashanti,* had been the objects of heavy torpedo attacks by the fleeing German ships. *Huron,* forced to turn sharply out of line to evade some enemy torpedoes, saw one pass down the starboard side and another on the port side. She resumed station and then turned out again, this time to slash back at the enemy with some of her own destruction-dealing torpedoes.

A grim sight loomed suddenly out of the darkness ahead. It was a destroyer, with flames leaping up her bridge and mast, crossing astern of *Haida.* Legs straddled to maintain his balance in front of her bridge, a signalman flashed steadily with an Aldis Lamp.

It was *Tartar,* limping along while she fought her fires. The enemy salvos she had taken had started a galley fire

144

which had sent the flames leaping up her lattice mast and over the bridge where a number of her ship's company, including her Captain, had been wounded in the first fierce exchange. Seven, including one officer, had been killed outright. Following astern, supporting *Tartar*, came *Ashanti*.

As *Haida* swerved to port to avoid her the stricken destroyer passed across her stern, in front of *Huron*, now speeding up to resume station astern of *Haida*. The burning ship was an awe-inspiring sight as she passed, less than a cable-length away.

Concentrating their fire on the two German ships fleeing to the Westward, *Haida* and *Huron* swept on, into the fiercest barrage of enemy fire they had ever known. The time was now fifty minutes past one o'clock.

The two fleeing Germans had got a head start Westward. They seemed to be comparatively undamaged and they returned the fire of the two Tribals with interest, concentrating first on one side and then on the other. *Haida*, leading, was illuminated by their starshell and they threw everything they had at her. Shells whined and screamed over her bridge and ahead and astern of her. Others, landing in the sea close alongside, sent fountains of water leaping high in the air and spraying over her bridge and decks.

An added menace now threatened her, from somewhere well astern, on a bearing about ten degrees off her starboard quarter. Close alongside, level with her bridge on the port side, observers saw a shell strike and carom off the sea. It had come from the bearing astern.

As they watched they saw a starshell burst in a trail of smoke on the port side and flood the ship in its eerie light. It had come from the same quarter and was followed by further salvos which were falling much too close for comfort. If *Haida* and *Huron* had fought hard before they were

145

fighting desperately now, their blazing guns sending an almost continuous stream of shells crashing at the enemy ships.

These ships were fighting back hard. Slashing at *Haida* came a series of salvos which swept in low. Whistling in directly over the tubes where the crews were crouching, the shells crashed and exploded in the sea alongside the engine room, blasting a great dent in the plates and sending splinters tearing through into the engine room itself. Spouted up by the explosions, a tremendous fountain of water crashed down on the afterdecks, soaking the unfortunate tube crews.

Up forward another near miss tore a jagged hole in the bow plates and another, bursting in the air just off the bows, sent a blast over the bridge which tore the Captain's steel helmet from his head, punctured his eardrum and left the inside harness of the steel helmet dangling like the tassel of a toque. Too intent even to notice it, he bent over the voice-pipe conning the ship.

Suddenly the engine-room telephone light on *Haida's* bridge began to flash steadily: the sound of the buzzer being lost in the din of battle.

"Bridge Engine Room," said a steel-helmeted officer, swiftly picking up the receiver. The voice at the other end, muffled by his ear protectors and the fearful noise of the guns, sounded faint and distant.

"Engine Room Bridge," came the engineer's report, "a splinter hit through the engine room hull has caused some damage. A pipe has been cut and we will not be able to repair it for about twenty minutes."

"Bridge Engine Room," called the bridge officer, his voice urgent, "is the damage serious?"

"Engine Room Bridge," answered the distant-sounding voice, "the damage is not serious. The hole is above the waterline, not more than four or five inches across. We hope

146

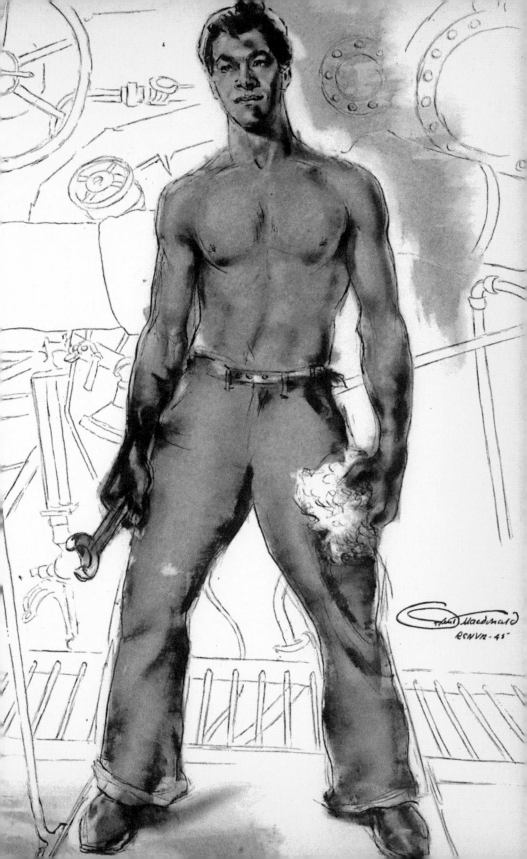

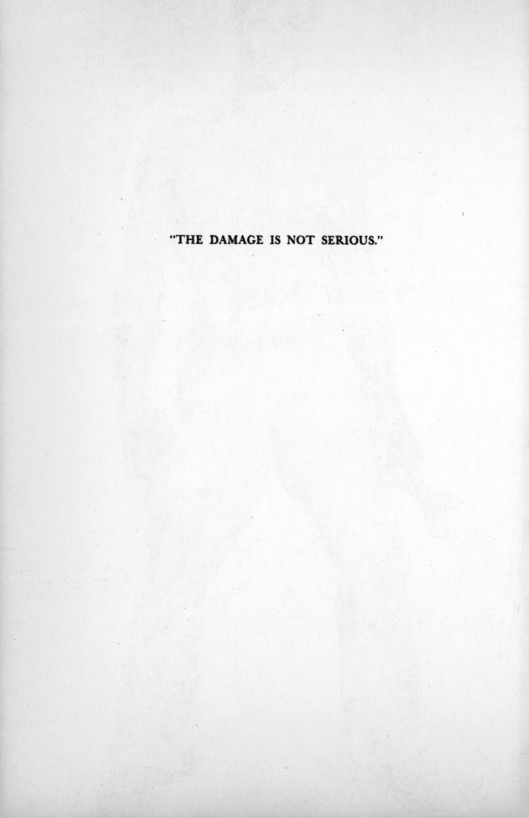

"THE DAMAGE IS NOT SERIOUS."

you don't need smoke-screen until we get it fixed. Twenty minutes should do it. Roger."

Hanging up the telephone the bridge officer reported immediately to the Captain. "Splinter hit in the engine room, sir," he shouted.

Seeing the Captain's look of interrogation the officer immediately added: "No serious damage, sir, but they can't make smoke for twenty minutes and hope we won't need it meantime."

The Captain smiled grimly. "It doesn't look as though we'll require it," he said, turning away to look at the enemy through his binoculars again.

Observation was tricky tonight. The clouds were so low that the Tribal's starshell, bursting above them, did not give any visible illumination until it had dropped below them. By this time it was so low that the interval until it dropped into the sea was very brief. Driving rain and spray, combined with splashes thrown up by near misses, kept clouding binoculars so that they had to be continually wiped clean.

The volume of fire from the guns of the two Tribals was terrific. Sweating ammunition parties passed shells up from hand to hand as fast as they could go. And the guns were getting hits. Again and again observers spotted the telltale red glow as a hit was registered on the fleeing enemy ships.

But the Germans were fighting a perfect gunnery action, weaving skilfully under cover of their smoke screen and using every trick in the book as they sought constantly to open the range. The Tribals, out for blood, maintained their fire. The enemy ships were fast and the only hope as the range increased was to get in a lucky hit in a vital spot and slow them down.

Far astern gunfire had broken out again but this time it was *Ashanti's* guns which sent their reverberations across

147

the water. *Tartar* had finally fought her fires to a standstill and was now wiping out the last traces of the flames. A German destroyer, apparently the one hit hardest in the first melee, had endeavoured to make to the Westward but intermittent fires had slowed her down and she had been observed by *Haida*, well afire and some distance astern. Slashing at this ship with salvo after salvo, *Ashanti* was setting her aflame from end to end.

What appeared to be an enemy signal was intercepted, asking, "Who is burning?"

From another enemy ship came a deprecating, "Sometimes it is me."

Haida and *Huron,* hoping that the burning one was up ahead, swept on in steady pursuit. There was a break in the clouds now and observation improved. They could see their salvos crashing all round the enemy ships and it seemed it would only be a matter of minutes until they made a real hit.

The Germans however had taken all they could. The Tribal gunfire was too hot for them and they made off at their best speed to open the range. Their course, unfortunately for the pursuers, led straight into a British-laid minefield which *Haida* and *Huron* were forbidden to enter. The pursuing Tribals skirted along the northern edge of it before turning back, so close that *Huron* actually sighted one of the ugly monsters less than fifty feet off her bows.

Haida led the way around now and they turned eastwards towards *Tartar* and *Ashanti* after losing contact with the two German ships. There was no point in a probably fruitless chase round the mined area and then on for miles towards Brest when the enemy ships had gained such a lead. They could only hope that the Germans might hit one of the mines.

148

Actually, as they were pulling clear their detectors picked up the sound of a heavy underwater explosion. They hoped it was one of the German ships.

The burning German destroyer was now distant on their starboard bow as they made to the eastward. She had been abandoned by her crew and *Ashanti*, finding her hard to sink by gunfire had hauled off, and was striking at her with torpedoes. They ran true, smashing home amidships just below the waterline with an immediate and singular effect. Across the water came the roar of a truly tremendous explosion which reverberated for miles and lit up the whole area of sea and sky in a wild unearthly glare. On the bridges of *Haida* and *Huron*, miles away, it was momentarily light enough to distinguish faces quite clearly. Plainly visible too against the light was the dark silhouette of *Ashanti* as she made to the North-East, away from her victim.

That was the end of one enemy ship. She heeled over and slipped under the surface then, the flames dying as she went. *Haida* and *Huron*, racing back to rejoin, got a contact ahead and, just as the last flames went out, observers on *Haida's* bridge glimpsed a ship approaching from the North-East. She appeared to be coming at fairly slow speed, not making more than fifteen knots. As *Haida* spotted her she altered course slightly to pass close on the port side on an opposite course.

From somewhere in that direction the second division of the 10th D.F. was known to be approaching. Up ahead somewhere too was *Tartar*. Not far away to the Eastward *Ashanti* must be around. It was a difficult situation in which to place the different ships. This ship coming in might be *Tartar* and her signal equipment would probably be out of action. She was coming bow on and, beyond the fact that she was a destroyer, the poor visibility made it impossible to

149

identify her superstructure. She gave no sign of recognition and the Captain did not hesitate.

"Challenge her," he ordered.

Haida's bridge crew watched intently. In a night encounter as confused as this, with friendly ships coming up it behooved one to be careful.

The Yeoman of Signals rested his lamp on his left arm and flashed the challenge. It had been only a matter of seconds since the unidentified destroyer had been sighted. The two ships were very close now with the stranger swinging to starboard and, from the churning water under her stern, apparently picking up speed.

From a signal lamp on her high bridge flickered an immediate acknowledgement of the challenge. It looked as if the answer was "six six", though perhaps the signalman had merely jiggled the key. As quickly as she had come into view she swept out of sight, a smoke screen showing where she had disappeared.

"Narvik, Roeder Class," called the observers as they caught a look at her superstructure in that last few seconds.

"Port fifteen, executive to Huron," ordered the Captain and the two R.C.N. Tribals swung in pursuit. From *Huron*, which had a contact on the unidentified ship but, though in station close astern of *Haida*, had not obtained a glimpse of it, so poor was the visibility, came a signal questioning if it might not be an enemy ship. *Haida's* executive signal confirmed her doubts. It was an enemy all right and a big one.

It was one of the strange and almost unaccountable things that can happen sometimes in night actions. The German ship, probably the leader of the enemy force, had mistaken *Haida* for one of his own ships coming up and *Haida*, despite the fact that all her guns were trained on him, had been

150

unable to get in a shot owing to the doubt as to identity as they flashed past each other.

The enemy Captain's optimism must have received a nasty jar right then, for, as *Haida* swung round and her guns could be brought to bear her Captain wasted no time.

"Open fire," he ordered.

The brief interlude from the close of the first fierce engagement had given a little respite to battered eardrums and strained nerves but now the roar and crash of gunfire shattered the night once more. The two R.C.N. Tribals, balked of a successful conclusion on their last targets, had no intention of letting this one escape and they went after her grimly, cancelling the signal made to *Tartar* that they were rejoining, with another that they were in contact with the enemy again. The time was now fifty-four minutes past two.

CHAPTER XIV

Haida to Tartar: *Am engaging one enemy destroyer.*

To the powerful Narvik had gone the advantage of the start and she made good use of it, opening the range widely in that first few minutes. It was going to be a chase that would call for quick and accurate thinking.

Huron, providing the illumination for both Tribals, opened fire now with starshell, revealing the German destroyer steering to the South-East. Both Tribals immediately engaged with main armament and the Narvik returned their fire.

Behind her smoke screen the big German destroyer, aided by the poor visibility, was making every effort to shake off pursuit. By her constant alterations of course and the widened range she was a difficult target.

If, as was suspected, she had been hit during the initial encounter, which would seem to be the only adequate explanation for her having lingered there so long afterwards, she appeared to have made good most of her defects. Her speed seemed irregular but it was high, and her gunfire was heavy and accurate.

At seventeen minutes past three *Haida* ordered Cease Fire. The range was too great for much hope of accuracy and the expenditure of ammunition did not justify it. *Haida's* Captain had been forming his own conclusions about the Narvik's intentions and had formulated a plan which he now proceeded to put into effect.

To maintain their present course would bring them into both British and German mined areas. The Captain believed that the Narvik, figuring she would be expected to attempt escape towards Brest, was really making for Cherbourg. If that was the case they could head her off, close in to effective range and fight it out with her.

Silence settled over the Tribals again and they drove through the rain-squalled darkness on a new course. In the Chartroom the Captain, bent over the plot, studied the chart and calculated the course.

Up on the bridge officers and men peered intently at the dark waters racing past on either side as the unmistakable smell of fuel oil came to their nostrils. With it were fumes that smelled like kerosene.

"Survivors! At green two o," called a starboard bridge lookout.

They were about thirty feet off, the nearest in the white foam of the bow wave which was washing over their small rafts. A small flare was burning on one raft and as the seas from the racing Tribals swept over them the men could be plainly seen. They were a soaked, half-clad, miserable looking crowd, hanging half on and half off their rafts. From farther out came the reedy note of a whistle by some endeavouring to attract attention. There appeared to be at least fifty of them.

Ashanti must have passed the same group during the night. Later *Haida* heard that a cockney member of *Ashanti's* Y gun crew, hearing the Germans hollering for help, looked over the rail and said: "Well you hadn't ought to have joined up, see!"

The bridge and deck crews looked at them impersonally as the Tribals swept past. They had come looking for trouble and they had got it. They were the enemy. Meantime there was a grim and urgent business in hand which allowed no time to pick up survivors.

One member of *Haida's* crew however decided that this was something needing attention and he promptly jumped overboard and was last seen making for them, whether for

153

peace or war will never be known. It was the whiskered mascot, Able Seaman Bunker.

The continual crash of gunfire had greatly excited him during the action. Scenting the oil, he had raced up the starboard side and stopped, peering intently at the water. Seeing the survivors, he growled menacingly and then plunged overboard after them. That was the last of Bunker. He was a seagoing dog.

Course was altered at half past three to avoid a minefield. Ten minutes later *Huron* sighted a horned mine on the surface and course was altered again. All contact with the Narvik had been lost and *Haida's* bridge crew wondered, as they drove through the darkness, if the Captain's calculations had been correct. What if she changed her mind? Their shells had crashed home on at least three enemy ships this night but they wanted the satisfaction of putting a definite end to one, as *Ashanti* had done. Nothing less would satisfy them.

Their probing instruments picked up echoes to the northward now. These, they knew, would be the ships of the second division.

Four o'clock came and passed. The minutes dragged with agonizing slowness. If their calculations were correct they should be closing in on the Narvik now, on a course that would enable them to surprise their powerful adversary and slash him with their salvos out of the dark. The element of surprise here might be the deciding factor.

The bridge crew were tired. A jug of cocoa would have been most welcome, for the men had been at their confined stations since ten-thirty the previous night and on their feet the whole of the previous day. The strain of continued action was taking its toll, but no man could be spared at this stage from his post. Action, if it came, might flare with startling suddenness.

At twenty-two minutes past four their searching instruments located a faint echo, distant on the starboard bow, and as they classified it their faces relaxed with satisfaction. The Captain had pulled it off. All alone, believing herself secure from pursuit, the Narvik was making for Cherbourg.

Altering course, *Haida* and *Huron* began to close the range. One of the leading ships of the second division had come up and was steaming on a parallel course some three miles to seaward. Both *Haida* and *Huron* were aware of her but were concentrating on the job in hand, believing she must be similarly aware of them, when she fired a sudden starshell which, bursting above and between them, revealed both ships as they raced along.

She, of course, had been completely unaware of the fact that the Narvik was inside them towards the land, and that she had given away their position.

The big German had seen them all right, for her guns barked and she altered course to the Southward immediately at a speed of more than thirty knots. The time was thirty-one minutes past four. It was now or never, and *Haida* and *Huron,* opening fire with their main armament, went after her.

His cherished escape plan foiled, the German leader put up a smoke screen and immediately attempted to double back. Actually had he held his original course at top speed he would probably have made good his escape. His last manoeuvre brought him well within range of the Tribals' guns. Driving through the seas at their utmost speed and concentrating on the Narvik with all their guns, the Tribals gave her no respite. Desperately she altered course again to the Southward to escape their fire, but the French coast was looming close now and she had little room left to manoeuvre.

It was a relentless fight. They were hitting her, though observation was difficult and they could not tell how hard, but her gunfire was erratic, switching first to *Haida* and then to *Huron* and hitting neither, and was slackening. At one minute to five she turned back into her smoke screen and was lost to view just as their last starshell was fired by the Tribals.

For a moment the awful thought that she might yet escape them gripped *Haida's* observers. She was the most elusive German they had ever encountered and a mistress of the art of evasion. With all their starshell gone it was possible, unless they could locate her quickly, that she might still get away under cover of the land, protected by shore batteries.

The loom of the false dawn was in the skies. Inshore they could see the lighthouse of Ile de Bas. The trailing smoke screen was spread along the sea in front of the lighthouse like a morning mist. The Narvik's last known position had been well to the right of the light and they strained their eyes at the smoke screen there, looking vainly for traces of her.

However one pair of eyes was keener than the rest. Searching the smoke screen on the other side of the light, the Officer of the Watch detected a darker shadow there, and his delighted shout directed their attention.

It was the Narvik all right. Moving slowly, she had doubled back under the smoke screen, hoping to evade detection under the land. Salvo after salvo slashed at her now as both ships concentrated their full armament on the target. *Haida's* first was short but the second was a good hit, and fire blazed on the enemy's decks. There was no need of starshell now. The cold, gray dawn was breaking. Turning, the Narvik tried to evade them again but she had no more sea-room. Desperate, to avoid sinking, she drove ashore as the Tribals raked her with salvo after salvo.

Just as she was striking the beach three signal rockets flared up from the Narvik's bridge, two green and a red, the same signal made by the Elbing driven ashore on April 29, and apparently calling for aerial cover. It was her last observed action, as *Haida* and *Huron*, steaming in as close as they dared, made sure that she wouldn't be sailing any more. To seaward the other ships of the flotilla, all of which had come up now, watched them give the enemy ship the coup-de-grace.

As *Haida* and *Huron* turned away to rejoin, the Narvik was heavily afire and intermittent explosions were racking her hull. So ended the leader of an enemy flotilla which had put to sea with high hopes of wreaking damage to the invasion lines.

As the 10th D.F. formed up and stood away two Ju. 88's, apparently in response to the Narvik's last signal, droned angrily out from the land and flew up their lines. The quick hail of anti-aircraft fire from the alert ships discouraged them, however, and they turned away and went back in over the land by Ile de Bas.

The tired Tribal crews relaxed now. The attack on the invasion lines had been met and defeated. Two enemy destroyers were finished and two others damaged, how seriously they were to learn later. Their own damage, considering what they had come through, was surprisingly light. *Tartar* would need a new mast and some other repairs, and *Haida* had a few holes here and there, but that was all.

Ships of the second division had been unlucky in having been unable to come to close action throughout the night, apart from a brief crack at the Narvik which fled northward in the initial stage of the action. They had done a good job of support, however, and had always been in reserve in case the action had gone against the first four Tribals. They remained on patrol now while the others went back to be patched up and reammunitioned.

CHAPTER XV

Proceed alongside to refuel, reammunition, effect repairs and make ready for sea.

It was a more contented ship's company which stood to stations on foredeck, maindeck and quarterdeck as H.M.C.S. Haida entered Plymouth with her battle ensign flying. They had practically the whole harbour to themselves and they remarked the contrast from their last sailing a few days before. The great invasion armada which had filled the reaches had all cleared for the shores of Normandy.

They felt it could now be justly said that "they had taken part". Messages of congratulations from Supreme Headquarters, from friends among the bombarding cruisers and other sources on their fine showing had heartened them. It was good just to be back. Here they had friends and here they could relax awhile from the constant strain of sea routine in the narrow seas outside.

This day as they sailed up harbour they were privileged to see an unusual and historic sight. The English pride themselves on being a phlegmatic race, not lightly moved to demonstrations of emotion or sentiment. It was a characteristic of theirs which, as the Tribals knew from their own observation, was largely true.

To the people of England, however, had come many strange and stirring sights in recent days. Right on their front doorstep they had watched the gathering of the mightiest invasion force in history. On June the sixth, culminating almost five years of war which had been fought around their shores and over their towns and villages, they had seen the flower of their youth and manhood set forth

159

with their ships, planes and guns to carry the flag of liberation to the lands where it had been suppressed so long.

That the landings had succeeded and the beach-heads established they knew, but there were many here whose eyes turned constantly towards the great empty harbour or looked beyond to the Channel seas, wondering what price might have been paid or what grim procession might come into view as the first of the ships returned.

To them the sight of the scarred but jaunty Tribals coming back from the battle was irresistible. Many English men and women, walking on Plymouth Hoe and along the roadways by the edge of the harbour, strangely devoid of uniforms for the first time in years, forgot their self-control and English reserve as they crowded to the seawalls to cheer themselves hoarse; waving and shouting with joy to the ranks of seamen drawn up on the decks of the battle-marked destroyers.

It was a moving and memorable sight. They wanted so much to express themselves; to voice their thankfulness for the success of the invasion, and this was the first tangible opportunity they had found. These were the first of the fighting ships to return and come within sight of their eyes and reach of their voices, and they let themselves go unrestrainedly.

The seamen in the ranks looked up and smiled back and waved to them. The sight of a ship coming in to safe harbour from the sea was a feeling they could understand, for to them it was an old familiar story and one that they lived again and again; but it pleased them to see this appreciated by the people of the land.

For the Tribals the stay in port was brief and busy. Refuelled, reammunitioned and with patches welded over the holes in their hull they were ready for sea again within a few hours. The main invasion was well under way but con-

160

"THE STAY IN PORT WAS BRIEF AND BUSY."

stant patrols were essential to secure its western flanks. Then too they were required as a covering force for the strong anti-submarine groups of destroyers, frigates and corvettes which were combing the Channel waters for the U boats now desperately attempting to break through the barrier of screening ships and planes.

Many of these anti-submarine groups had been drawn from the North Atlantic forces of the Royal Canadian Navy. Making up and down the Channel, it was not uncommon for the fast-moving Tribals to sight many old friends operating from Ushant and the Lizard up to Dover Straits. During one eight-hour period they sighted *Restigouche, Skeena, St. Laurent, Chaudière, Saskatchewan, Kootenay, Swansea, Meon, Alberni, Kitchener, Prescott* and several others. It was like being on the "milk run" out of Newfoundland.

One sunlit afternoon, as *Haida* lay in the outer harbour in Plymouth, at a buoy they were coming to know rather well, a military launch came alongside. Up the jumping ladder climbed a Major, a sergeant, a corporal and two privates.

A few minutes later they were followed by a Lieutenant and after him a miscellaneous assortment of signalling apparatus was hoisted to *Haida's* deck. Seamen watching these new arrivals spread a wild flood of buzzes which circulated with amazing rapidity around the ship. There was no enlightenment until later.

Towards sunset *Haida*, in company with *Huron*, slipped her moorings and headed out through the seagate, bound on a secret and mysterious mission. At sea, to a select volunteer audience of several officers, two P.O.'s and four seamen ratings in the wardroom, the Major expounded the plan.

They were to be "the voices" of an invasion force, passing words and signals over the Major's equipment that would

161

lead the enemy into thinking an amphibious operation was about to make a landing on the western coast of the Cherbourg peninsula. This, it was hoped, would have the effect of drawing off some of the forces now defending Cherbourg and facilitate the Allied entry into that great seaport. Allied planes would lay down a bomb barrage at the start of the operation.

The Major, who indicated he was attached to the staff of the Commanding General, was a very pleasant man and a keen soldier. Being out of his own field he did not quite appreciate the hazards of the operation which he had requested of the navy.

The sailor's admiration for the soldier is deeply and sincerely founded but when army strategists tackle naval operations the sailors are inclined to shy away. To the army, naval operations are a highly technical and thoroughly unfamiliar field.

At a superficial glance it looked like a simple operation. All the ships had to do was to proceed to a designated spot off the French coast and help to create a diversion. To the seamen, however, it was not so simple. To get to the area they would have to pass through exceedingly narrow, heavily mined waters guarded by shore batteries. It would be the same coming out. While the signal voices did their stuff for the enemy to pick up they would be more or less stationary for twenty minutes in the most dangerous area of all.

The sea is a comparatively flat surface. Objects picked up on it by enemy shore radar could be accurately determined. The number, type of ships, course and speed could readily be plotted. How then could two destroyers simulate an invasion force?

As the news got around the ship in more or less garbled buzzes it was received with mixed feelings. Messdeck law-

162

yers, arguing both for and against the army, got really busy on it. Red, getting tired of being asked if he wanted to run up a wired and bombed beach to kidnap a German General, which was the idea conveyed by the latest buzz, quizzed the Bluenose Killick.

"Is it on the level?" he asked. "Are we really going to make an imitation landing with fifty men and capture some Krauts?"

The Killick however was not to be drawn. "All I know is that we got to imitate landing signals," he informed Red. "I heard nothin' about a landing. If the Old Man says you guys gotta land then we gotta land an' that's all there is to it."

"Steel helmets and Lanchesters for all anti-submarine ratings an' stokers," suggested Red looking over the bunch in the Mess. "We won't need you guys if the ship's going to lie off shore. An' don't be alarmed. We'll cover you with Y gun. The Krauts won't get you. If anybody does it'll be us."

Radar ratings, always proud of the efficiency of their equipment, encouraged the dimmest view. Knowing they would pass within easy range of enemy-occupied territory, they predicted that shore batteries would be busy.

"Aw we'll be six or seven miles off," suggested Joe.

"An' what good will that be?" asked a Radar man. "You all know what happened off the Gironde. They were straddling the ships when they were seventeen miles out. That's radar!"

"No chance," said the Killick shortly. "The Yanks and the R.A.F. are giving these guys such a pounding they won't know whether we're friends or enemies. All their radar sets are probably pounded out or pointing straight up by this time."

163

It could be a tough show. On that the men were agreed. If however the army thought this scheme would make the capture of Cherbourg any easier, then the men were willing to concede that the Navy should take up the army's burden to this extent and do what they could.

It was a bad night for the army. All hands off duty were catching a couple of hours' sleep while the ships were crossing the Channel. The Major had been accommodated in a bunk, the owner of which was flaked (stretched out) fully-dressed on a cot just beyond the loose curtain which gave the Major privacy.

Haida had taken a new mascot on board. The antithesis of Bunker, it was the smallest dog they had ever seen. An affectionate little thing, it loved to play. Nosing around aft about ten-thirty it discovered the officer asleep on the low cot and, scenting a friend, immediately proceeded to snuggle up to him.

A former merchant service man, this officer had known ships with rats. Waking, and thinking some rats must have come on board *Haida,* he flicked his torch on and looked around. Finding nothing he went back to sleep. The little dog, waiting patiently behind his head while he moved a-round, tried again. This time it clambered up on his chest and attempted to lick his face. Like a train set suddenly in motion a number of things happened with bewildering rapidity. At least it must have seemed that way to the little dog.

Believing as he wakened the second time that a large and cheeky rat was using his chest to make faces at him, the officer acted promptly. Bringing his left arm up across his chest he batted that rat in a way that was intended to put it far from his vicinity.

It caught the poor little brute squarely on the side and

164

sent it on a quick parabola through the air. It fetched up against the loose curtain and this, bulging inwards, braked its flight but decanted it neatly off one side onto the face of the sleeping Major, the first solid substance the little dog's frantically searching feet could find to attempt to steady on.

Thinking by the feel of the object he had batted with his hand that this must be a somewhat large rat, the officer rose and flicked on the light, just in time to see the small, discouraged-looking dog scurry out under the curtain and disappear.

In the bunk there was a wild commotion of flailing arms and muffled grunts and the Major, half smothered in loose blankets and his heavy coat, rolled over the side and hit the deck, three feet below, with a far from gentle thud as he endeavoured to disentangle himself.

"A rat! Great big one tried to get at my throat. Think I've got him in the blankets here," he yelled, hastily disengaging himself and stepping back.

While the officer watched him, he vigorously trampled the blankets and his overcoat under his heavy boots and then gingerly shook them out.

"Must have got away," he muttered and felt his throat tenderly with his hand. "Have you a mirror?" he asked.

"Right there," said the officer and pointed to one nailed to the bulkhead.

"By Jove, he was close," said the Major. "Look at the scratches on my neck. Do you have many rats here?"

"It's rather difficult to say, Major. They vary quite a bit. Depends on where you've been of course," the officer added in explanation.

"It was a very large rat that attacked me. He seemed as big as a cat," said the Major. "Are all the rats here like that?"

165

"Some of them are quite large," admitted the officer. "However I don't think he really meant to attack you. Sometimes they get cold and try to snuggle in beside your head. They don't like the foot of the bed. This fellow may have seen a cockroach walking across your neck and tried to knock it off just as you wakened up. They don't like cockroaches."

"Good Lord," said the horrified Major, "what a frightful way to live. Doesn't the Admiralty do something about these things?"

The officer shook his head sadly. "I'm afraid, Major, they just refuse to worry themselves about anything like that. Of course they say there's quite a few around the Admiralty itself," he remarked and brightened up quite a bit. "Makes the old boys up there feel at home, as if they were back at sea, I expect."

Seeing the Major was in a mood for conversation, he warmed to his subject. In the next half hour the fascinated army man heard about Maltese rats, "Gippy" rats, Russian rats, English rats and their characteristics. He heard how they were often tamed; about the Admiral who carried one in his pocket up on the bridge and how it would run up his jacket and lick his face. That rat loved him.

Then there was the Leading Cook who kept a pet Maltese rat with beautiful fur and pointed ears. He used to spend hours grooming it. One cold night it burrowed down in some dough for warmth and was finally served up in the duff, alive but completely hairless. The history of seafaring rats was well on its way when the insistent ringing of the buzzers sounded for Action Stations.

The ships were closing the land now and the bridge watch took up their Action Stations. It was very dark, with low visibility. One humorist commented that if the shore

166

"THE SEAMEN DIDN'T LIKE IT."

batteries opened fire on them it was so dark that they wouldn't see any shells landing unless they arrived on deck. There were planes around. It was hard to tell whose they were.

In line ahead the silent, darkened ships entered the narrow waters and steamed steadily towards their objective. They were within range of the first enemy shore batteries now and the watch on deck was alert and observant. Nothing was sighted, however, to cause alarm and shortly after one-thirty they closed in towards the mainland itself.

Up ahead, where the darker bulk of the land loomed against the night, things were getting under way. The bombers had arrived and were beginning their work. From their ringside position in the ships the sailors watched with interest. It was a magnificent panoramic view of night aerial battle.

Along the height of land and further inland the bombs were falling with steady precision, sending up great blasts of flame where they landed. In one place quite a large fire was burning, showing plainly on the coastal ridge. Enemy tracer, arching up into the skies, was seeking the planes. Searchlights were being switched on and pointed upwards. One powerful beam swept across the water and elevated, it seemed, just before reaching the ships.

Nothing came their way at all. Whether it was because the shore batteries and radar installations were too busy with the planes the sailors did not know. From the great parachute flares being fired into the skies by the Germans to spread a weird and lurid light above the land, it appeared they were looking for paratroops and hoping to illuminate them and machine-gun them in the air.

The army men did their stuff with the volunteer voices helping, while the men on deck watched the magnificent pyrotechnic display above the fiercely contested peninsula. Whether the Germans were tuned in to pick it up or not they did not know. When it was finished and their time was up, the ships withdrew as quickly as they had come. As they cleared to seaward they passed so close to one of the enemy-held Channel Islands that they were within a few feet of the blue-lighted offshore buoys, hardly a mile or so out and could see the dim bulk of the island right abeam.

Once in the clear, in the wider waters of the Channel, the Major returned to the cabin where he had rested previously. There, after a welcome cup of cocoa, he was cordially invited to bed down for the remainder of the night.

"Won't be light for three hours yet," his host informed him. "No point in you staying up when you don't have to. Why don't you turn in and I'll give you a call in time for breakfast before you go ashore."

Despite his satisfaction in the night's operations there was a harried look in the Major's eyes, and he declined the invitation with thanks. "No thank you. Really couldn't sleep," he said, and was last observed to have set his chair facing the door so that nothing could approach him without being seen.

Over a cup of coffee in the wardroom his erstwhile host, in company with the Engineer Officer, the Gunner T and the Navigator, engaged in animated conversation. The new mascot was with them and every once in a while one of them would stroke it, murmuring delightedly, "You great big bad rat you," while the little dog happily wagged his tail.

168

CHAPTER XVI

Am in contact with submarine previously reported by R.A.F. Liberator.

Allied armies, investing the Cherbourg Peninsula and threatening northwestern France, had disrupted enemy communications and the Germans, as a consequence, increased their sea traffic in the confined waters of the rockbound St. Malo, Channel Islands and Cherbourg area. Their E boats, no longer able to operate from Cherbourg, had been forced to move their base upchannel to le Havre.

This latter move freed the Light Coastal Forces of the Plymouth Command from much defensive patrol duty and they were now operated on the offensive in this area as weather permitted.

To the Tenth Destroyer Flotilla went a dual role in the same theatre. They were to provide support to the M.T.B.'s and M.G.B.'s of the Light Coastal Forces in the event of their encountering opposition which might be too heavy for them and also to seek to intercept and sink any enemy shipping which might attempt to pass to the westward of the Minquiers.

On the night following the diversion created by *Haida* and *Huron* off the Cherbourg Peninsula, the first success in the new area was achieved by *Ashanti* in company with the Polish destroyer *Piorun*. Encountering a force of five or six German "M" class minesweepers, armed with three-inch guns and heavy anti-aircraft armament, *Ashanti* and *Piorun* sank two and heavily damaged two others among the shoals.

The patrols were maintained. On the night of June

169

23rd, *Haida* and *Eskimo* were in this area, but encountered nothing worthy of attention during the night although quite a few aircraft were around. As most of these were R.A.F. planes hunting surfaced U-boats and using Leigh Lights to illuminate suspected targets, it behooved one to have recognition signals handy.

One plane was heard approaching *Haida,* diving low as she came, and then the Leigh Light was switched on, bathing the ship in its eerie, bluish brilliance. The Yeoman of Signals jerked the rocket identification release signal for this period of the night and the three coloured rockets flared off. The plane switched off its light and hurriedly answered the signal.

The seamen didn't like it. For a prowling destroyer on the hunt for targets it was not so good. Hostile eyes could have observed the incident and taken precautions. With the element of surprise lost the hunting would be poor. However, it didn't happen often, which was a consolation to the seamen.

As the ships came out into the Channel the following morning they passed Roches Douvres lighthouse in full daylight. This was an enemy-manned lighthouse situated on a series of low reefs some miles off the mainland. One wondered what the German keepers must be thinking as, after four years of practically unchallenged occupation, they saw the Tribals, the first destroyers which had ventured in these waters, pass boldly less than three miles off. It must have looked like the writing on the wall to them.

It was a bright sunlit day. The ships had orders to carry out a patrol down channel which would bring them between the Lizard and the Scilly Isles. In that area they were to provide support for anti-submarine groups of frigates and corvettes working in long, slow, intensive sweeps

170

for U-boats, much to the disappointment of certain racing fans on board who had hoped to be in Plymouth.

Being Saturday, dog-racing day in Plymouth, some humorous moans were heard from the dog enthusiasts over the tea table that afternoon.

"What ship is always at sea on Saturdays?" asked a gunner, standing up and striking an oratorical attitude.

"*Haida!*" yelled everyone present.

"What ship is always in harbour on Saturday nights?" was the next question. Flotilla leaders being what they are, that one was answered unanimously too.

"What we need is a union," continued the orator, "yes sir, a union. Here we are at sea night after night and now what do we get?"

"More sea!" yelled the audience.

"That's right," beamed the speechmaker. "Now I ask you, how can I pay my mess bills if I can't get to the dog races to make money?" With that he thumped the table dramatically and looked searchingly at his audience in the approved oratorical style.

"Do you pay your mess bills, old boy?" asked a Lieutenant cuttingly. "I thought you always borrowed the money."

The Paymaster Lieutenant, who had been thoughtfully sipping his tea and who was responsible for the collection of all wardroom mess accounts, looked up brightly as he heard them mentioned.

"All mess bills are due on the tenth of the month following and that's positively the last date," he announced.

"Hooray!" cheered the wardroom members who were paid up.

The orator, who had maintained his stance through this sideplay, subsided into his seat with a groan. "How can they do this to me?" he enquired of the company at large.

There was an interruption at the entrance and the Signal Officer, a cheerful individual, came in, tossed his cap expertly towards the settee and slid into a vacant chair.

"Hi chaps," he said, "just heard some news that'll interest you." He searched for a teapot that still contained some tea and the gentlemen of the wardroom gave him their attention.

Nibbling a biscuit he kept them waiting for a moment before he spoke. "Remember those survivors we passed the night of the *Narvik* show? One of our escort groups picked them up next morning. They got a hundred and twenty German survivors in that bunch. They had been drifting on their rafts off the French Coast all night and were damn glad to get a lift."

"What about Bunker?" came an almost simultaneous query from several of those present.

"Yes, I was coming to that," said "Sigs". "I'm afraid we've had Bunker. There was absolutely no trace of any dog to be seen and, according to the survivors, they hadn't had a glimpse of one either. Actually I heard about this right afterwards, but I waited until I got a chance to talk to one of the officers in that group before I passed it on."

"When do we go in?" asked the dog enthusiast.

"Almost any time now I imagine," said "Sigs", "but I'm afraid you've had your dogs this trip."

He had barely finished speaking when the reverberating clang of a distant underwater explosion sounded against the hull.

"Depth charge!" yelled the Anti-Submarine Officer, and with one accord they made for the ladder to the maindeck. As they went, the insistent buzzing of the anti-submarine signal sounded throughout the ship. She heeled over as she turned and increased speed.

172

On the maindeck there was orderly confusion as men, running to their stations, nimbly avoided each other. There was a lively interest in their eyes. This was something different for the fast-stepping Tribals.

Up on the bridge, the Officer of the Watch described what had happened. Indicating an R.A.F. Liberator up ahead, manned by a Czech crew as it was later ascertained, he told how the plane had sighted a diving U-boat and dropped a depth charge after it as the Nazi went under in a fast dive. Circling now, the plane dropped a smoke bomb to mark the spot where the U-boat had dived.

Haida and *Eskimo* closed to investigate, slowing down to submarine-hunting speed as they neared the area. Beside their equipment ear-phoned specialists operated their instruments and listened carefully, making the most of the unusual opportunity.

"Definitely classified as submarine contact," came the first report to the waiting bridge crew and the Plot. *Eskimo* had got the contact first and carried out an immediate attack. Swinging wide, *Haida* came around and increased speed as she steamed towards the plotted contact to carry out an attack. Depth-charge parties were alert. As the order came to fire, the projectors sent their big cans hurtling to port and starboard and other charges went over the rails from the racks.

The water here was two hundred and fifty feet in depth, a bad spot for a U-boat to be caught in, and she seemed to be at the bottom. The charges had been set for that depth. As *Haida* steamed clear there was a moment of waiting and then the sea astern erupted violently.

Observers scanned the area thoroughly, but no traces of oil or debris could be seen. Returning, the ship plotted the location again and *Eskimo* moved in swiftly and let a depth-charge pattern go. The two ships were quite close and the concussion of high explosives sent up great geysers of water and seemed to shake the surface of the sea.

Slowly and steadily the two ships worked on the contact as one hour crept past and then another, *Haida* directing and *Eskimo* depth-charging. The two Captains began to have doubts. If this was a U-boat it must be a tough one to resist attacks like these in such shallow water. Seven patterns had gone down on her but she still appeared to be immovable at the bottom. It began to look as if it was a submerged wreck. There were lots of these in the Channel.

If it was to be a long-delayed operation then it would be advisable to call in one of the escort groups and turn it over to them. Actually the High Command back in Plymouth were considering the advisability of doing this and letting the Tribals continue their patrol. An examination of the position, however, showed that an escort group would shortly be in that vicinity in any case. The switch-over could be made when they were sighted by the Tribals.

Haida moved in and carried out another attack and *Eskimo* followed up. A very small oil-slick showed on the sunlit waters, but that could easily come from a submerged wreck blown apart by depth charges. At gun mounts, men idled and waited. This was not the kind of action they were accustomed to.

Shortly after seven the Captain decided to send all hands who could be spared down to supper. The ship was liable to be at Action Stations all night if they continued on patrol and, as they had been on patrol duty throughout the previous night, it was advisable to let the hands have their supper as soon as possible. The Bridge and half the guns remained at Action Stations while the others took time out to eat.

174

As cooks and stewards had all been at their Action Stations the men off duty had to wait while supper was prepared. The sea alongside was covered with nice-looking herring which had been stunned by the depth charges and soon, armed with cans attached to long poles, the waiting men got busy hooking them inboard.

Contests automatically developed between different sections for this welcome addition to their diet. One bunch were leading with a haul of nineteen fish when a sudden cry of "Submarine!" sent all hands running back to stations.

The Bridge had been warned by the anti-submarine specialists a moment before that the U-boat was apparently blowing her tanks, a preliminary to coming up. She was surfacing all right, driving up with her engines going.

Ahead, slightly to starboard, about seven hundred yards off the bow there was a sudden flurry of white water as part of her bow and conning tower began to emerge simultaneously.

From *Haida's* starboard Oerlikon batteries came a quick reassuring burst of fire as the gunners steadied on their target, and opened a devil's tattoo along the U-boat's hull and conning tower.

Up she came until her bows, showing her two uppermost tubes and her long hull, was above the surface. She seemed to be down a bit by the stern. B gun, depressed and firing almost abeam over open sights, went off with a concussion that rolled the ship, making several hands wonder if *Haida* had been hit.

Ranged too short, the first salvo sent up fountains of water between the ship and the U-boat, which was being swept constantly by close-range fire. B gun fired again and this time it was right on target. Tearing into the submarine at the base of the conning tower, it was a direct hit

175

which caused the red glow of fire to show in the U-boat's ripped interior, and smoke began to pour from her.

Eskimo was firing as she came in and a salvo thudded into the U-boat's hull. She came right up until she was almost touching the U-boat and then eased astern a little as she saw the Germans were jumping into the sea.

The submarine was sinking and her crew were abandoning ship, coming up through the after hatches and jumping into the sea. Seaboats had been lowered by both destroyers and were pulling towards the spot, hoping to be able to board. It was a losing race. The U-boat heeled slightly and then slipped quietly under, stern first, leaving only a white flurry of foam swirling on the surface to ia' the spot. Three hours' depth-charging and three minutes of gunfire had ended her story, the first bringing her to the surface and the second sending her smashed and broken to the bottom.

Survivors were bobbing up everywhere in the area now. Each one appeared to have an individual yellow inflatable raft. These had been inflated and the Germans were resting on them, half in and half out of the water. The whalers closed in among them and started to pick them up. Motor cutters were lowered by both ships to speed the rescue as the survivors appeared to constitute quite an impressive number.

Eskimo, being nearest the scene, stopped and received the majority of prisoners picked up by all boats, while *Haida* carried out a protective sweep and search against a possible mate to the sunken U-boat.

Haida's motor boat brought back to *Haida* the last survivors to be rescued, an officer and six men, when she returned to be hoisted aboard. With them the motor-boat crew brought several German liferafts. The Captain had signalled them to pick some up, having always wanted one for fishing in some of his native Nova Scotian lakes which have never had a boat on them. He later traded one to the Commanding Officer of H.M.C.S. Prince Robert, who was also an ardent fisherman, in return for a case of sherry.

There was no fight left in the Nazis. One of them, on being taken into the whaler, had opened his arms wide and said, "Sieg Heil! Sieg Heil!" A prod in his ample tummy from a tommy-gun in the hands of a grim-looking stoker and a growled order to "Siddown!" made him subside hurriedly.

Several men, veterans of North Atlantic convoys, had leaned over the ship's rail and jeered at the Nazis in the water. "How do you like getting your own dose?" they yelled. They had seen too many merchantmen torpedoed and their crews thrown into the icy waters to have any sympathy for these killers.

When it came to getting away, the Germans had not been slow. The hail of fire which had swept their craft must have effectually stifled any ideas they might have had about surface fighting. Fifty-one of her crew of fifty-two had been picked up by the destroyers' boats. Of these, twenty-seven were wounded, mostly when they were abandoning ship.

Under questioning it developed that they had sailed from a Norwegian port some weeks before and had been ordered into the English Channel to attack the invasion lines. So intensive there were the anti-submarine defences of searching surface craft and planes that they had been unable to surface for the past forty-eight hours. When, getting desperate, they attempted to do so in daylight, the plane had chased them under and then the destroyers had attacked.

They said they had been hit by every depth charge pattern which the destroyers had dropped. Leaks were started in the hull which they were unable to close and finally, up to their waists in water, they had made a dash for the surface.

177

In three years of operations it was the worst depth charging they had experienced.

They were well supplied with cigarettes and emergency rations. The rations did not look very satisfactory, but the cigarettes were apparently made in the United States and were a brand called "North Star", probably stores which had been accumulated prior to the war, or captured since. They were in airtight tins.

They were not an impressive-looking crowd. One of them had been wounded by splinters in the leg. He was laid out on the table in the Captain's day cabin, utilized as an emergency Sick Bay, and bandaged up by the Surgeon. He never ceased to stare his hatred, though, for a Nazi superman, he was far from being anything worth looking at.

The escort group had hove in sight now but no assistance was required of them. The daylight was fading to dark and both Tribals had been ordered to land their prisoners at Falmouth and then proceed to Plymouth after refuelling sufficiently. Setting course they proceeded on their way.

It was about two o'clock in the morning when they arrived off Falmouth Harbour and a fine drizzling rain was falling, making harbour buoys particularly difficult to distinguish. They found the entrance all right and followed the twisting channel up harbour to the naval pier, alongside which they berthed.

Despite the late, or early hour, their coming had aroused considerable interest. It was not often that fighting ships as big as these found their way here, and quite a few heads could be seen peering down through the rain to look at the ships in the faint light of two blue battle lamps.

An army guard had arrived for the prisoners but, unaware of the number arriving, they had concluded the total was probably five or six and that a sergeant and six men would

178

be sufficient. Transfer of prisoners ashore was delayed until a sufficient guard was turned out and ambulances brought down to take the most seriously wounded.

Aboard the ships few hands turned in, most of them preferring to stand around and watch the proceedings. Around four o'clock, both ships slipped their moorings and stood away from the dim-lit pier in the rain. Feeling their way down the dark harbour they passed out through the gate to the open waters of the Channel again and made course for Plymouth. Not until then did the hands off duty turn in.

Coming up harbour on their arrival they received quite a welcome, signal after signal coming in from ships as they passed. From one of the cruisers came: "Congratulations! Elbings, Narviks and U-boats all seem to come alike to you. Well done!"

From another destroyer in the 10th D.F. came a wryly humorous query asking if this was quite decent. To that one the Captain replied, "We have to do something on Saturday afternoons."

All hands at liberty went ashore that night and celebrated. Getting the U-boat gave them a personal satisfaction even greater than their victories over the enemy destroyers, and they were heartily glad to have put one out of action. Even the dog-racing enthusiasts allowed they'd trade their favourite recreation for a U-boat any day.

CHAPTER XVII

Ships of the 10th D.F. will carry out operational offensive as directed, sweeping approaches to port of Lorient in Bay of Biscay.

The Navigator, a frown of concentration on his face, was completing a bunch of corrections. The ship was at sea, sailing down the English Channel in broad daylight, with the coast of Cornwall in plain sight. Up here in the chart-room, high in the Bridge superstructure, it was quiet. Each time they made harbour a bunch of new corrections invariably came aboard. They referred to new minefields, swept channels, wreck buoys, changes in flashing lights and such-like maritime intelligence in both friendly and unfriendly areas. It was the Navigator's duty to see that the necessary corrections were made on the charts concerned.

"Ah-hah!" exclaimed a voice, and the smiling face of a brother officer appeared round the door.

"This is a private office. Why don't you knock and then listen to me telling you I'm busy and can't be disturbed," said the Navigator rudely.

"Ah-hah!" repeated the other, in no way abashed, "he shuns the society of common men. He must be an admiral indeed, Effendi Pasha himself — and the telephone booth, just what were you doing in there for more than two hours all alone? And what about the little Wren who cut herself on the barbed wire after dark and had to get her leg bandaged. Who chased her over the barbed wire anyway, and who claimed to be a doctor when her leg was being bandaged?"

"We're at sea now and that's all behind us," remarked the Navigator grinning reminiscently. "The boys exaggerated it. All that happened was that we found an old bottle-green

180

"ALL HANDS AT LIBERTY WENT ASHORE."

tail coat with gold shoulder ropes in a cupboard in the hotel. It must have been a hundred years old. I put it on, and then I was introduced to a foreign officer as a neutral admiral. He fell for it.

"You can imagine how I felt when I found he had invited two of his bigshot pals to have dinner with us. They wanted the lowdown on what I thought about everything."

"You told them?"

" 'Well I no spika da Inglese ver goot. Oi yust coom by Asia Minor. We fin oot who win then we go major.' That kinda shook them. We got really confidential then and invited them up to the room to play Asiatic games. They turned that down and couldn't wait for their coffee. Going out of the hotel they were looking over their shoulders."

"You son of a gun! How about the Wren . . . what happened to her?"

"Oh she tripped over the barbed wire on the esplanade after dark and they brought her into the hotel. Ask the Doc and the Engineer about that. They looked after her. We all had a lot of fun . . . just good clean fun."

"Sure," agreed the visitor, "only the way we heard about it, you were all as high as kites. Stinko in fact, just able to function and that was all. You should have seen the three of you coming aboard. You looked like 'Hangovers Incorporated'."

"That's just the trouble here," commented the Navigator gloomily. "A few hard-working sailors go for a run ashore for a couple of nights, have a few watery beers and a little harmless fun that even a fond mother couldn't take exception to, and look what happens. You fellows have us imitating Admirals and getting stinko."

"O.K. It was just a church social," agreed the visitor in the weary tone of one who has heard everything now. "I

181

didn't come up here about that. Now that you've conde-
scended to come back to the gentler side of war and return
to sea, tell me, my pilot, just what we're doing going down
the English Channel at ten o'clock this bright morning.
The ship resounds with strange buzzes. Whither goest we
and on what quest? Is it North America or the Spanish
Main? The messdeck buzz says we're escorting Mr. Churchill
to New York and then going to South America to intercept
Hitler's getaway."

"Take a look for yourself," said the Navigator, indicating
the chart on which the course was laid off.

The other did so and emitted a long, low whistle. "So,"
he said. "We're really going round the corner and into the
Bay of Biscay. That looks interesting. How many ships
are with us?"

"Just two. Tartar, Blyskawica and ourselves. Deep water
and a long way from base this time."

"I think I go back to my cart and get some sleep. It looks
like all-night Action Stations and maybe all-day too. Goodbye, Pilot. You'll probably be arrested when we get back
but don't let that influence you. If you run us aground I'll
testify against you."

Pulling the door shut just in time to intercept an Admiralty Manual of Navigation intended for his head the
visitor departed.

"These V.R.'s," muttered the Navigator darkly.

Haida was hopeful of getting into action again. June
had been a good month for the 10th D.F. *Huron* and
Ashanti had closed it off with a spirited encounter with
three well-armed enemy trawlers in the Channel Islands
area. The brisk engagement in the rain-squalled darkness
of a stormy night had ended with two of the trawlers going
to the bottom and the other limping off badly damaged.

182

Tartar and *Ashanti* celebrated the fourth of July by hammering four enemy tank-landing craft under the guns of Lannion Harbour. Four nights later *Huron* and *Tartar* had braved the defences off St. Malo to engage four enemy trawlers and got in some hits before the shore batteries forced them to retire.

Allied land forces were thrusting westwards from the Cherbourg Peninsula and threatening the enemy-held Channel ports. The naval forces, now extending their sphere of operations to the Bay of Biscay, were seeking enemy shipping moving between French Atlantic ports in the Bay itself. It was on this duty that *Haida,* with the British destroyer *Tartar* and the Polish *Blyskawica,* was now bound.

Haida's company had been fortunate enough to secure sixty hours' shore leave while the ship was held in harbour for engine repairs and boiler-cleaning. On this, their first shore leave since long before D-Day, they had relaxed somewhat. The Captain had located some good fishing on a Devon stream; the First Lieutenant and several other officers had gone to London; and the Navigator, in company with three other officers, had sampled the wartime delights of an hotel on the Cornish Riviera.

Just what had transpired there was still the subject of interested questioning in the wardroom. It was apparent that a good time had been had by all. The hotel was full of uniforms of different services from different countries, and it was claimed that these guests had required some looking after.

The *Haida* group had been very tired the night of their arrival, so tired that the Navigator had gone to sleep in the telephone booth while phoning a friend in Newcastle. Unaware of the local situation inside the booth, a long queue formed up waiting to phone and was there for over an hour

183

before another member of the party, also waiting in the queue, decided to investigate and found his shipmate fast asleep with the phone in his hand.

Two of them were said to have been horrified at the sounds of gaiety coming from a room where a party was in progress after midnight. They knocked sharply on the door. Inside the room there was a sudden silence and the door remained closed.

"This is the Manager speaking," called one through the door. "There are people in this room who are not registered. If they do not return to their own quarters in five minutes they will be asked to leave the hotel."

As the pair retreated to the end of the corridor they claimed to have been almost overwhelmed in the rush of people who emerged following their ultimatum. This the wardroom flatly refused to accept, claiming it as a nasty thing to do because they had probably been refused an invitation to the party.

Sunset over the Atlantic was rather magnificent that evening. It seemed somehow comforting to look to the Westward across the seas knowing the skyscrapers of New York were over there on the long coast of North America and that only the seas rolled between. The day had been an agreeably lazy one for both Watches in their periods off duty. They had enjoyed their meals and the gossip over the leave experiences. All hands were rested and fresh. As the twilight faded and the ships turned towards the blacked-out coast of France they buckled on their gear and readied for the long night at Action Stations which was ahead of them.

The wind was from the South-West, but the night was dark and clear as they closed the land. They were in line ahead, following a weaving course in the wake of the leading destroyer. Aircraft were around, and for a while it looked

184

as if they were being shadowed from astern, but this was incorrect. No planes had located them.

Midnight came and passed and the Force swept steadily nearer their objective. About half an hour after midnight flares were sighted low above the surface and some seven miles to the southward. They were probably dropped by planes searching for U-boats.

On the Bridge everyone was in high good humour tonight after their leave. This new adventure down into the Bay was pleasing to them. They liked being out in the deep waters again, away from the narrow seas of the Channel, and this raiding operation had aroused their interest. They were veterans at night-fighting now.

The light on Ile de Groix, an island off the coast, came in sight at half-past one. Searchlights were sighted shortly afterwards, over where Lorient lay, going on and off at intervals. This seemed to be a lively area and the Bridge Watch were alert and vigilant as they scanned the waters and endeavoured to determine what might be doing.

Time passed more swiftly now. On board the raiding ships the crews tensed, ready for the sudden action that might flare at any moment if the enemy discovered them first. Two o'clock came, and seven minutes later they saw flares, followed by heavy anti-aircraft fire to the Northwards. Friendly planes must be attacking in that area.

The waters here were more sheltered, almost flat calm, and the smell of the land was heavy in the air. Gone now was the freshness of the ocean breeze. This was a new and untouched area for raiders from the sea. The Germans had held undisputed mastery for more than four years in these coastal waters.

Twenty minutes later, as the ships sped on their swift searching way, *Tartar* picked up a contact. *Haida* got it a

185

moment afterwards, then another and another. It seemed to be a small ship convoy. Swiftly the information was passed to the Plot and the position, course and speed of the enemy charted and relayed back to the Bridge.

The leading destroyer heeled over as she led the way around, manœuvring into the best position for attack. Speed was reduced to give the gunners every opportunity to do their stuff to the best advantage. Below decks the ammunition supply parties, their flash helmets, gloves, mouth masks and lifejackets on, had passed up shells until an unbroken supply line extended from the guns to the magazines.

On top of the tubes crouched the Torpedo Crew, silhouetted against the darkness of the night. Theirs was a grandstand view. Muffled against wind and weather they waited, ready to train the tubes to any ordered bearing and send their messengers of death speeding through the seas to the target.

Three o'clock came and the ships were in position to attack. Up ahead came a crack of gunfire that raised every head. It was *Tartar,* opening fire with starshell to illuminate the enemy.

"Ignite," ordered the Captain, and *Haida's* X gun mounting spat fire.

Under the dark night sky, to starboard off the bow, the shells burst their eerie brilliance over the waters beneath them and showed up the enemy ships.

There were four of them, looking like small merchant ships and showing their sterns as they headed towards the land. The range was two miles. Selecting the right-hand ship as her initial target, *Haida* opened fire.

The third salvo was a hit and others followed rapidly, thudding home and raking her hull. From two of the enemy ships came a quick and well-directed return fire. Starshell,

186

right on range, burst above the Tribals, illuminating them with the greenish glow characteristic of the type of shell used by the enemy.

High explosive burst overhead, unpleasantly close, and the Bridge Crew ducked their heads instinctively.

"Here comes tracer right at us," called an observer, and most of the Bridge Crew crouched down, seeking cover behind bearing indicators or anything handy. Only the Captain remained upright, conning the ship.

The Navigator, crouching down by the compass, turned up the collar of the raincoat which was his invariable dress in action and smiled impishly at an observer squatting beside him.

"A lot of protection that'll give you," remarked the observer.

"Don't spoil my illusions," returned the Navigator.

The tracer petered out and the heads bobbed up again. The first ship was pretty well shattered by *Haida's* gunfire and fire was shifted to the second, another beam-on target apparently not yet being engaged by the other destroyers. She appeared to be a small merchant ship towing some kind of barge.

The first salvo arched just over her amidships but the second was a direct hit. Between seven minutes past three and nine minutes past three she was hit with every salvo and appeared to be a complete wreck above the waterline.

A check to see how the other ships were faring showed that the left-hand ship, which had put up a very spirited resistance, was having her fire smothered now and was being raked repeatedly by *Tartar's* guns. *Blyskawica,* firing vigorously at the same target, was putting up a good show.

"Check fire," came the order and the guns were silent as they swept up the second time. The merchant ship and her

187

tow were still afloat and *Haida* opened fire on her again.

Several hits in quick succession saw her beginning to founder and fire was shifted to the tow. This was an exasperating target. Hit repeatedly, it stayed afloat and it wasn't until the Officer of the Watch laughed suddenly and called out, "It's a B.P.T.," that it dawned on the observers what they were engaging. It was a battle practice target and it was living up to the reputation of battle practice targets nobly.

Fire was shifted to the remaining ship which had previously been engaged by *Tartar* and *Blyskawica* and it was now hit heavily. Between half past three and twenty-five minutes to four *Haida* raked her repeatedly until she was seen to founder and start under.

It was all over then, and the destroyers formed up and stood towards the open sea at thirty knots. It was twenty minutes to four. The action had been short, sharp and decisive, the enemy convoy having been wiped out close to their own base. A few survivors clinging to liferafts and boats and one battered battle practice target were all that remained to tell the Teutons what had happened. To the listening ears of the French people in that area the roll of gunfire to seaward would be significant. It meant that the ships of His Britannic Majesty were taking the offensive in these hitherto enemy-held seas, harbingers of liberty to come.

CHAPTER XVIII

Force 26 will carry out offensive sweep in French Coastal waters as directed.

Inshore a hill loomed, rising steeply from the water's edge. The narrow strip of beach at the foot of it was much frequented by the fair sex, in the person of W.A.A.F.'s and A.T.S. girls from adjacent air and A/A gun stations. In daytime it was a popular bathing rendezvous, a circumstance which contributed to considerable dereliction from duty on the part of the signalmen. When their glasses should have been watching the signal station or other ships they were focused too often on some luscious damsel daintily testing the water temperature with one foot. Loving couples came under their scrutiny too, a play by play description of the progress of some soldier's evening romance on the hillside being a hot news topic.

Now, however, the night had come down and it was dark and silent under the stars. Here in the outer harbour, dimly discernible in the starlight, many ships were moored. In this particular corner of the bathing beach were the buoys generally used by the ships of the 10th D.F. and they had come to look on the area as their own. Three of them on this calm night were moored to a buoy and tied snugly together.

No lights showed. The Watch was on duty on *Haida's* blacked-out decks. Down below the hands on board were turning in, looking forward to the privilege of a night's sleep in harbour, when the Duty Officer and his party, making "rounds" to ensure that all was well above and below, came through the messdecks.

Pausing at the entrance to a lower-deck mess, the "rounds"

party considered the unusual scene which met their scrutiny. A young seaman, looking youthful enough to pass for fifteen, was kneeling by a locker seat in prayer, the light shining on his upturned face. The other men in the mess, their heads uncovered, watched him in silence. A card game had been left with the cards on the table and a cribbage game abandoned half way through.

With a quiet "We'll look in here later," the D.O. (Duty Officer) carried on, somewhat amazed. That was undoubtedly the toughest mess in the ship, as he well knew.

"It happens every night sir," volunteered the Leading Seaman.

"How come?" queried the D.O.

"The lad lost his mother, sir, some years back. His father and he were very close, his old man trying to do double duty to make up for his mother being gone. Then the war came an' his father had to join up. Before he went overseas he made the lad promise to say his prayers every night like his mother taught him an' told him to do, before she died.

"The kid got lonesome an' as soon as he could make it he joined the Navy. After training he was drafted here. He tried to keep his promise but he took a lot of kiddin' an' got discouraged. This ship's got quite a reputation an' he was scared.

"The Killick in there is a tough case. He had figured the kid had to learn to take it, but one night he saw him turnin' in without sayin' his prayers, an' lookin' miserable. He asked him why an' got wise to the whole story. The Killick told the mess then what the score was an' made the kid climb out an' say his prayers proper. There was no more kiddin'.

"Now they're all with him. They check up to see that he writes his dad regular and they put in a line themselves to

190

"EYES AND MINDS WERE TURNING HOME."

let the old man know the boy's O.K. The kid's hopin' his old man gets leave soon an' comes down an' visits all his friends in the ship."

"That's quite a yarn," commented the D.O.

"You know, sir," confided the Leading Hand, "this is a strange ship. I've served in corvettes, escort destroyers an' cruisers but I never seen a ship like this before." There was a note of pride in his voice.

"What's different about it?" asked the D.O.

"I don't just know, sir, but there's something about her that's different. The whole bunch of us an' the ship herself are like one. The officers and men are different. I don't mean they're not pusser navy style. They can be plenty pusser when they have to be, but there's a kind of understanding about them where being pusser is concerned. They're a tough lot, the toughest bunch of officers and men, taking them by and large, I ever seen, and there isn't a man aboard who would trade this ship for any other ship in any navy. She's a lucky ship, it's true, but she's got a kind of able viciousness when she's fighting that makes her seem like she's alive. An' she can fight.

"The other ships know about it too, sir. One of the R.N. ships said the other day they'd rather sail with this ship than any other one in the Flotilla. They always feel good when she's around."

"Sounds like she's a real Haida Indian all right," conceded the D.O.

"She sure is, sir," agreed the Leading Hand.

Whatever she was, the time had come for her to be tested again. It happened down the Bay. Operations had been extended there, with the sea forces now operating in coastal waters from Ushant to the Spanish Border. The cruisers

191

had come back to the Command following their D-Day operations and, in addition to *Bellona* and *Diadem*, the six-inch Uganda Class cruiser *Mauritius* had arrived for duty.

Following an extended foray by *Diadem*, *Bellona*, the escort carrier *Striker* and the destroyers *Tartar*, *Ashanti*, *Haida*, *Huron*, *Blyskawica* and *Piorun* of the 10th D.F., supported by the River Class destroyers *St. Laurent*, *Chaudière* and *Kootenay* for anti-submarine duty, the situation obtaining in the waters off the French Atlantic coast had been carefully studied and close blockade ordered.

In support of this policy *Bellona*, in company with *Tartar*, *Ashanti*, *Haida* and *Iroquois*, was ordered on a foray intended to interfere with enemy shipping which might be attempting to move between Brest or other northern ports and the Gironde. *Huron*, *Haida's* faithful running mate since *Athabaskan* was lost, had been relieved for refit and *Iroquois*, spick and span after a long refit, had come to take her place. The men were sorry to see *Huron* go. She had earned universal respect in the Flotilla as a good, steady ship and a thoroughly reliable running mate. They would miss her.

Following the usual procedure the ships kept over the horizon, well off the land, as long as daylight lasted. When darkness fell they turned in towards the coast and the crews went to Action Stations. The moon was coming up, a ruddy moon that shone fitfully through scattered, slow-drifting clouds, and there was a slight haze on the calm surface of the inshore seas.

The warm, heavy smell of the land was strong in their nostrils as they sailed in between Belle Ile and Ile d'Yeu, making for the mainland. If any evacuation of key men and technicians was attempted by sea from the U-boat bases it was through this area they would have to sail southwards.

Shortly after midnight as the ships combed steadily on their searching courses they had the first alarm.

"Stand by," came the order from the Bridge and gun crews and supply parties came to quick alertness. The leading destroyer had reported a contact. One by one they confirmed it and then, heeling over as they went around to form in line ahead, they moved in to attack.

"Here we go again," said the Navigator as he reached for a steel helmet. "What a ship!"

With a crack like a gigantic whip the cruiser's guns broke the night silence, and observers on the speeding destroyer's bridges ranged their binoculars on the suspected bearing and waited for her starshell to burst and reveal the position.

Low above the distant horizon the starshell burst and its eerie light illuminated the waters there. Black objects, looking like toy ships at that distance, showed beneath it.

"One trawler! One minesweeper! One coaster!" called the observers.

Other ships also were suspected to be around the area, and *Iroquois* was ordered to provide additional illumination as *Haida's* guns and her own opened fire. It was forty minutes past midnight. *Haida's* first target was the trawler. Four minutes later, hit by repeated salvos, the German ship was flaming from stem to stern and *Haida's* guns shifted to target number two, an "M" class minesweeper. The other ships were busy and several additional targets had been discovered. It seemed to be a convoy of at least nine ships, escorted by well-armed minesweepers and trawlers.

Three minutes sufficed to set the second target well alight and at three minutes to one she blew up. Carrying on up the enemy line *Haida* observed a coasting vessel burning furiously from the fire of the other ships, and opened fire on her third target.

This was a fair-sized merchant ship of about four thousand tons. Ships in line ahead of *Haida* had raked her with a few salvos and *Haida* continued the good work. As the shells tore into her the watching observers saw great chunks of her upperworks torn loose and hurtled into the sea. She had a single, very tall funnel. It teetered crazily and then crashed overside as a salvo smacked in amidships. Sparks shot up through the deck where its base had been and then the red tongues of fire showed through the smoke.

Observers on *Haida* saw another ship sinking at four minutes past one, a victim of gunfire from the cruiser and other destroyers, and then, as they had reached the end of the enemy convoy, the destroyers altered course together and turned back towards it. The enemy were fighting, but some of them, when they saw the grim avengers closing in on them, seemed to lose heart and start to abandon ship.

For target number four *Haida* finished off a damaged coaster and then raked a minesweeper with repeated salvos until she was considered destroyed. It was twenty-eight minutes past one now. *Haida's* searching guns found a stopped coaster at close range and battered her until she capsized and rolled under.

Force 26 had gone down the enemy line again and now, forming astern of *Bellona*, they went back at the doomed convoy.

Four burning enemy ships were visible on the surface as they closed. Steaming past these they finished them off one after the other and then went after still more targets, picking up enemy ships which had scattered and tried to escape after the first attack.

The smoke of battle was hanging low on the hazy seas. Starshell hurtling through the clouds and illuminating the scene would show up a ship through gaps in the billowing

194

smoke from burning enemy craft, and the ships of the Striking Force would open fire. Then, just as the flames rose on *Haida's* seventh target, there was an explosion close on *Haida's* quarter.

Tongues of flame rose up close at hand and the Bridge Observers realized to their alarm that the flames were coming from *Haida's* own quarterdeck. Increasing in volume and leaping angrily upwards, their flickering light was reflected in the seas alongside as the ship steamed on steadily, and to each man's mind came the sudden memory of a night in April. It had been just like this that *Athabaskan* had looked after being hit.

The quarterdeck phone was dead when the Bridge Crew tried to find out what had happened. X gun position was tried next and the Officer of the Quarters there ordered to look over the apron and try to give the Bridge some idea of the damage.

A midshipman of the Royal Navy, one of those serving in R.C.N. ships on the exchange plan for experience, was Officer of the Quarters on X gun deck. An English lad some sixteen years of age and looking about fourteen, his voice had a high-pitched, cultured English accent. Acknowledging the gruff order from the Bridge he called back a moment later.

"I am very sorry, sir," he reported, "but I am unable to ascertain the exact extent of damage. Y gun appears to have been hit and is no longer in control. Two bodies, which appear to be dead, are lying beside the turret. Others are being taken out who are either dead or wounded. The turret itself is on fire and the Damage Control party are endeavouring to bring a hose to bear on it. That is all I could see and now, may I return to my gun, please? We are very busy."

"You may return to your gun," said the Bridge Officer hanging up the phone. "Extent of damage unknown, sir," he reported to the Captain. "Two thought dead and several wounded in Y gun. Y mounting out of action at present and on fire. Damage Control party fighting the fire now."

The ship carried on, her superstructure brightly illuminated by the flames from aft. On the Bridge no one spoke. A long minute dragged past and then the flames receded, flickered up, and then receded again. They were feeble now and then, as if a sudden hand had been clamped down, they went out. From the quarterdeck came the report that the fire was under control; two men were dead and two wounded seriously. Other casualties were light.

There had been heroism down there. One wounded gunner, his face blackened and his eyebrows burnt, a great gash over one eye and a steel splinter in the eye itself, had got out of the burning gunshield after the explosion and stared wildly around. Looking back and seeing his wounded mate still in mortal danger inside the turret he went back and hauled him out.

Meanwhile the action continued. Target number seven had blown up and fire was shifted to another target, a trawler. It was soon destroyed and it was noted, in the light of the starshell, that two large groups of survivors were in the water in this area. A burning "M" class minesweeper loomed through the smoke and she was raked with salvos until she was seen to be foundering.

That was the last target which could be observed. Forming up again the Striking Force swept to the northward. It still wanted more than two hours until dawn. The moon was shining intermittently through the clouds, taking on a reddish glow through the rising smoke as they left the battle area.

196

Down aft on the quarterdeck a working party was checking over Y gun but, with the barrels pointing drunkenly over the side, it was beyond immediate repair. Inside the after flat, a long line of men was forming to carry the ammunition from Y gun's magazine up to the forward mountings. It was a grim scene in the dim light of the battle lamps as the sweating, gear-encumbered men lifted the shells as they were passed up and, cradling them in their arms, made their way forward, going carefully through the after flat past the blanket-wrapped bodies of their dead comrades, lying on stretchers at the side of the passageway outside the Sick Bay. Inside, others were being treated for wounds and burns. A blood-spattered steel helmet, burst open along the length of its crown, lay beside one of the victims.

A young seaman knelt and picked it up. Tears were streaming unashamedly down his powder-blackened face.

"All right lad. You brought him out. You can't do any more," spoke up a stern-faced Petty Officer as he noticed the incident in the crowded flat. "He's had it, chum," added the P.O. and his grim visage softened for a moment as he saw the grief on the lad's face.

"He was a good guy, the best guy I ever knew," said the young seaman earnestly. "He never had no father or mother. He always said this is what he was made for an' that it was better for him to go this way. He laughed at everything. 'Laugh at it boy,' he used to say 'It can't ever get you down as long as you can laugh.' He's got a girl friend back home. 'She's only wasting her time having anything to do with a punk like me,' he used to say. He'd tell me these things. I knew him better than anyone else. He was my chum."

The big Bluenose Killick loomed up and held out his hand for the battered helmet. The lad surrendered it without pro-

197

test. "There's another Stand by coming," said the Killick, "Are you O.K. Joe?"

"Sure!" said Joe. "I'm O.K." His voice was steadier now and his eyes were losing some of the dumb agony of his grief.

"Let's go," said the Killick turning towards the quarterdeck.

Joe looked at the still, blanket-wrapped form on the stretcher. "Goodbye Red," he whispered, then he turned and followed the Killick.

It was thirteen minutes past three. The leading destroyer had detected ships moving close in under the land. They were obviously making for the adjacent harbour under cover of shore batteries. The enemy ships had the advantage of position but Force 26 wasted no time. They closed to attack at once.

Bellona's guns broke the silence as she opened up. Visibility was bad here but observers saw three and possibly four ships, all armed. *Haida* opened fire from both forward mountings and the action became general.

From the enemy ships came a brisk and well-directed return fire. It looked as if it was going to be a hot show. There was a shout as a hit was seen on an enemy ship and flames burst out on her deck amidships. Then there was a vicious "whurrumph!" as a high-explosive shell seemed to burst right above *Haida's* foredeck followed by a muffled explosion.

"A gun mounting out of action," came a report to the Bridge. "No casualties."

B gun mounting was bearing the load for *Haida* now with X gun providing starshell. Three minutes later another hit was observed on an enemy ship and flames once more showed through the smoke. The German ships were fighting

198

desperately as they reached in towards the land.

Over *Haida* an enemy starshell burst, fully illuminating her. It was an eerie feeling to the Bridge Watch to be directly beneath the revealing, greenish-tinged light with the enemy guns concentrating on her. A vicious burst of high explosive sounded in the air overhead, fortunately just over and then another just short, before the enemy starshell ended the interminable-seeming seconds by floating down into the sea astern and being snuffed out by the water.

It was over then. A misty dawn was breaking as the Striking Force formed up and stood to seaward. What was left of the enemy ships had reached the safety of navigational barriers which prohibited the ships of the Striking Force following, and the action had to be broken off.

Haida, taking her dead with her, made back for Plymouth. With two gun turrets out of action she needed the services of a dockyard to make her fit for sea again.

CHAPTER XIX

Investigate local situation at Arcachon Point and Les Sables d'Olonne, F.F.I. detachments reported active in these areas.

All hands on deck looked shoreward as the ship made in for the French Coast in the bright morning sunlight. The land was clearly visible and houses were showing up along the skyline. The sea was changing colour, the deep blue of the Bay giving way to the lighter blue of the shallower coastal waters.

Gun crews stood by their stations as *Haida*, her new guns trained and ready, led the way in. *Kelvin*, the R.N. destroyer with which she had been in company all week, followed close astern, *Haida* being senior ship.

It had been an interesting week: they had cruised the long Biscay swells, from Ushant down to that inner corner of the Bay where the mountains that are the dividing boundary between France and Spain come down to meet the sea.

The first night had been spent on patrol off Ushant, blockading the seaward approaches to the besieged seaport of Brest. All night they had watched the flashes from the guns of the two opposing armies, the flak and the bursting bombs from air raiders. There had been a great glow in the sky above the burning city, a reflection of the fires from the air raids and continuous bombardment to which it was being subjected. Nothing had attempted to escape to seaward, however, through the surrounding ring of fighting ships.

Heaving to off Ile d'Yeu they supplied the French Forces of the Interior there with some arms and promised to look in again later. Giving the German-occupied mouth of the Gironde a sufficiently wide berth to avoid shore batteries, *Haida* and *Kelvin* made their next landfall at Arcachon

Point. This was on the long reach of more than a hundred miles of low sand dunes which led up from the Spanish border on this section of the French coast.

French Forces of the Interior had been reported as having reached this area but the ships could detect no sign of them. The coast seemed silent and deserted, except for the wreckage of a plane which had obviously attempted a beach landing there and cracked up. No signals came off from the land.

Sailing south, keeping the coast in sight, they made the corner of the Bay next morning. St. Jean de Luz and other towns there made an attractive picture at the foot of the coastal mountains. The inshore waters were dotted with the sails of French and Spanish fishing craft. They were dotted with mines too, as *Haida* discovered when agitated French fishermen informed them they were sailing right over a German-laid minefield. The Germans had evacuated their border and customs garrisons here some days previously.

Heading north again during the night and remarking the unusual sight of brightly-lit ships, for the French and Spanish fishing trawlers in that vicinity were taking no chances of being mistaken for hostile craft, the two destroyers closed the land some thirty miles north of La Rochelle to investigate the situation at Les Sables d'Olonne.

A famous holiday resort in times of peace, this attractive Biscay town was built around a sandy-beached bay, its Grande Plage, or esplanade, extending for more than three miles along the waterfront. The harbour, with two stone piers extending seaward, was at the northern end.

The sunwashed yellow and white houses fronting the esplanade were in plain sight as *Haida* eased her way some three miles offshore, *Kelvin* screening her to seaward. Through the binoculars observers could see the upperworks of several sunken ships. People ashore could be seen moving around and gathering in clusters to look seaward.

There was drama in this moment. For the ships it was one of the objectives of the long years of fighting, the reward for the ceaseless patrols off the land when they could venture within sight of the coast only by night. This was another D-Day and it was all their own.

Tense and expectant, they studied the town across the sun-lit waters. If the Germans were here they could expect gunfire at any moment. Faintly to their listening ears came the rattle of small arms fire, a machine gun, but nothing stirred the water in their vicinity. The shooting seemed to be along the beach, among the entanglement of wire and wooden crosspieces erected on the sands as a defence against invasion.

Something was happening on top of a square stone tower overlooking the harbour. A flag was breaking out. Slowly it shook loose in the faint breeze and its colours were read eagerly. It was the red, white and blue of the tricolour of France.

A signal lamp stabbed its message from *Haida's* Bridge and from the tower came an answering blink. From out between the stone piers a wheezy fishing tug, crowded with citizens, puffed its slow, asthmatic way towards the ship. As it closed it could be seen that the people on board were all wearing the red, white and blue armband of the Maquis, the French Forces of the Interior, the fighting troops of France's underground.

Some were armed with revolvers and had German-type wooden-handled stick grenades thrust inside their belts. They all, including an attractive young mademoiselle in khaki shirt and skirt, with two bandoliers across her chest, wore berets.

202

Despite the ominous lowering of the barrels of *Haida's* close-range weapons which covered their craft continuously as it approached, the F.F.I. group broke into enthusiastic cheering as they neared the ship, shouting *"Vivent les Anglais!"* and holding up their hands with two fingers extended in the V for victory sign.

Coming alongside the quarterdeck practically all hands made a concerted rush to swarm up on the destroyer's low maindeck. This was gently but firmly stopped by a guard of cheerful seamen. Only the leaders of the party were to be allowed aboard. Five were chosen by the tug's company and they, accompanied by the pretty mademoiselle, who was said to be the local F.F.I. secretary and interpreter, came up the ladder and were escorted to the Commanding Officer's cabin for a conference. The others, somewhat disappointed at not being allowed up on deck, were soon consoled by packs of cigarettes, chocolate bars and other comforts, tossed down to them by *Haida's* friendly crew.

The delegation cheerfully asserted that the Boches were finished. *Kaput!* The last of them had just left the town. Interrogation revealed, however, that their cheerfulness was somewhat unfounded. The German forces had only been pulled back some seven miles to protect their supply line between the Gironde and St. Nazaire. The town of Les Sables was still cut off except by sea, and the enemy forces in the neighbourhood were several thousands of fully-equipped troops.

There was no lack of food in the area. Situated in a fertile agricultural belt, they had a sufficiency of meat, butter, fruit and other edibles. The inshore fishing was rich with lobster and all the common varieties of fish found in these waters. They were short only of coffee, tea, sugar and soap, apart from luxuries like tobacco. What they wanted principally was guns with which to fight the Boches.

Just how effective they might be against trained troops was anybody's question. Long since drained of its best men it was not to be expected that the district could produce much in the way of good irregulars. Willingness to fight, firmly expressed in spirited phrases on board a friendly warship, may be translated into something rather different when the speakers find themselves in the front line against the enemy. It is much easier to go "underground" by removing an armlet and burying a rifle than facing up to a well-armed and able enemy, particularly when one is no longer in the first flush of youth. Rifles are of little avail against a well-equipped army in the field.

However, there were good men among them, men who would face up to any odds for the ideal that was France, and one of them was the F.F.I. Commandant. He was a soldier and to him was entrusted a supply of automatic rifles and a machine gun, with all the ammunition that could be spared. Into the tug too went goodly supplies of tea, coffee, sugar, flour, jam and tobacco.

A landing party of two officers and a P.O. interpreter was detailed to accompany the F.F.I. craft and investigate conditions ashore. *Kelvin* added another officer and a P.O. As soon as they were aboard, the tug cast off and made in for the harbour.

As they neared the wrecks one of the officers asked what had happened and was quickly enlightened by a cheerful Frenchman:

"Un matin . . . trois avions de R.C.A.F. . . . Pom! Pom! Pom! . . . Zut! Des bombes ont entièrement détruit les bateaux!"

Up the channel between the piers was another wreck.

Queried about it, the Frenchman shook his head regretfully. That was the German's work. They did it to block the harbour, he explained.

The tug drew into a landing stage from which a long, iron-runged ladder led up to the dock. The Commandant excused himself and went up ahead to make arrangements. The naval party followed.

Quite a reception had been arranged. At least a hundred and fifty soldiers of the F.F.I. were drawn up in front of a building. As the naval men walked up the short pier the troops did a smart Present Arms! Five small cars were drawn up and the landing party got into them. A soldier with a tommygun sticking out the window sat beside each driver and another guard stood on the running board on the driver's side.

"Snipers!" explained a Frenchman briefly.

Avoiding the front esplanade the five cars drove rapidly towards the Southern end of the town where the F.F.I. headquarters were located in a hotel. Monsieur the Mayor and other dignitaries, including a uniformed Surgeon Commander of the French Navy, were waiting there.

The first move was to lay out refreshments. Bottles of champagne appeared like magic, glasses were filled and the party urged to partake. This was a day of celebration, they were told, and the Mayor was going to make a speech.

He looked like a man who had known many worries in recent years and he seemed to be very sincere. He spoke, of course in French but this is the gist of what he said:

"I cannot begin to describe the inexpressible joy that is in my heart today . . . how it moves me to welcome these gentlemen, the first of the forces of liberation who have come here to make us free men once more. It moves me deeply that some of them have come from Canada, from a great land

205

across the sea, to take part in the fight. It is a long way but they have come, along with our friends from Britain and my heart is filled with welcome and thanksgiving.

"They have given us arms and supplies. I can assure them that we will use these arms, to take up our part once more in the fight against the enemy. Messieurs, un toast . . . à nos libérateurs!"

"A nos libérateurs!" was the hearty response, and then the Mayor gave them another toast which was echoed with even greater enthusiasm:

"Vivent nos Alliés . . . Vivent la Grande Bretagne, le Canada, les Etats-Unis!"

Raising their glasses high, the Landing Party toasted their hosts in turn with a right good will:

"To France!" and "The French Forces of the Interior!" and downed their champagne.

The telephone rang and the Mayor was called to answer it. He appeared somewhat excited and, to the surprise of the audience, concluded the conversation by giving an emphatic "razzberry" into the telephone mouthpiece. Returning, he explained:

"That is what you call *le Commandant des Allemands.* He has heard that two British warships are in the neighbourhood and has warned me to have no intercourse with them. He threatens he will send in some tanks to clean up the town."

Ordering the glasses to be filled again he promptly proposed another toast, distinctly derogatory to the enemy. It was drunk with enthusiasm.

Very complete information was available here of the size and disposition of the German forces in these areas. The numbers were quite impressive, as was the area they were still in control of, which included the Gironde estuary, Bordeaux, la Rochelle, St. Nazaire and Lorient.

Leaving the F.F.I. headquarters the Landing Party was exhibited to what appeared to be a select gathering of local people, probably including the F.F.I. families. It was noticeable that a line of sentries with tommy-guns always stood between the crowd and the somewhat embarrassed sailors. They, being perfectly capable of looking after themselves, would have preferred the sentries withdrawn so that they could then have given the people a more spontaneous welcome.

At the harbour, information was received which was immediately signalled to the ship and in response to an urgent signal in return, the Landing Party hurriedly embarked again in the tug. Two German-manned armed ships, disguised as fishing trawlers were reported to be coming down the coast, making for the Gironde through inshore waters. They were said to be just beyond the next headland to the North.

Haida, waiting for the Landing Party, sent *Kelvin* off immediately to intercept them. As soon as the tug came alongside, and her own people were aboard again she followed swiftly.

Rounding the point she saw that *Kelvin* had slowed. What appeared to be two steam trawlers were steaming southwards some two miles offshore. As they watched, *Kelvin* fired a shot across the bows of the leading one. Disregarding the warning the trawlers carried on, apparently hoping they could still bluff their way and not reckoning just what they were up against. *Kelvin* opened fire immediately with close range guns and a stream of bullets sprayed both trawlers' decks and hulls.

The German crews stood not upon the order of their

207

going, all of them jumping over the side except a handful on one of the ships who tried to man a quickfiring gun mounted forward.   They died . . . suddenly, in a quick hail of bullets.

Kelvin went alongside one and *Haida* took the other.   As *Haida* closed, the bodies of two German seamen drifted past on the tide, their lifeless eyes wide open.   Other bodies lay huddled by the low, bullet-marked bulwarks.

Survivors were picked up and made prisoner.   The two small ships were well-armed, carrying anti-aircraft guns for'd and anti-tank guns mounted on rubber-wheeled carriages aft, as well as multiple mortars.   Prize crews were put on board them, and it was decided that the destroyers would each tow one back to Les Sables d'Olonne.   They would be a welcome addition to the F.F.I. forces there.

At eight knots the tows were got under way, but *Haida* had not proceeded very far before a shout from the prize crew in the tow drew attention to the fact that the captured ship was making water dangerously fast.   *Haida* stopped her engines hoping to bring the tow alongside and pump it out, but the prize had been too badly damaged by the gunfire and was sinking fast.

A sudden wild yaw to starboard brought her bow down to surface level and, like a tired swimmer, she slipped under, leaving the prize crew floundering in the water.

Rafts were let go hastily for the survivors to cling to and the whaler was swiftly lowered and pulled to their aid.   The water temperature was seventy-three and the sun was shining, so it was difficult to understand why the whaler's crew seemed to be slow in picking up the prize crew, some of whom seemed barely able to keep afloat.   Despite the fact that they were wearing lifejackets only their mouths and noses were showing above the surface and the little waves were washing over them.

The mystery was explained when the disgruntled whaler's crew brought them back to the ship and they were assisted on board. So bundled up with clothing that they were incapable of climbing the ladder unaided, they looked like men who had been specially dressed for a polar expedition.

"Why are you weighed down with all that gear?" an officer asked one man who had required the assistance of at least four of the boat's crew to bring him inboard. It was Dan, the lean Westerner.

"Sir, I bin four years in this war and this is the first chance I got to git my hands on some souvenirs," was the unblushing reply.

"He's got so much on he damn near drowned," said a Leading Hand. "Only the tip of his nose was showing when we hauled him out."

Once on board the prize, the Boarding Party had lost no time investigating what was to be found. To their amazed delight the trawler was packed with loot the Germans had brought from Brest: there were chests of high-ranking Nazi officers' uniforms complete with medals; cases of champagne, perfumes, silk lingerie and stockings; German leather flying suits and all sorts of supplies which they were just getting hold of when the craft began to founder.

Hastily donning leather flying suits and grabbing what they could in the way of medals, lingerie, perfumes, binoculars and other loot, the Boarding Party, looking like a bunch of pirates, abandoned ship somewhat sluggishly. As one observer remarked, they were afraid to jump in case they couldn't make the surface again so they let the ship sink beneath them and just floated off.

One rating, undressing on *Haida's* quarterdeck, took off

209

a leather flying suit, laid down two beautifully engraved Nazi dirks of the kind affected by Goering, unwound six pairs of silk stockings from around his neck and then divested himself of a German general's tunic complete with medals and a pair of German flying boots tied to his middle. All this, in addition to his own clothing, had been supported by a Mae West. Despite the fact that he almost drowned he had resolutely refused to abandon a single item of his loot and only regretted he hadn't time to gather a few more souvenirs.

Making back to Les Sables d'Olonne the ships left the other prize there, receiving an enthusiastic acclamation from many small fishing craft which had come out from the port. They had watched the two German ships making their way South but had been powerless to prevent them. The little action had seemed to these interested spectators a sea battle of some magnitude. However, the ending had been most satisfactory, for, the prize being left with them, they now had a navy of their own.

Heading northward again the ships checked with F.F.I. shore authorities at Ile d'Yeu and picked up seven German soldier prisoners there for transport to England. The Wehrmacht soldiery were more than glad to be taken off. One who turned out to have been the Nazi customs officer on the island for four years, was observed to take a cordial farewell of his captors. Checked concerning this, the F.F.I. said he had been a most reasonable customs officer, always turning his back whenever possible.

It was two in the morning before the two destroyers slipped into their anchorage at Plymouth, right astern of a white-painted German hospital ship marked with the Red Cross. This craft, of which there were suspicions, had been captured coming out of St. Nazaire and escorted to Plymouth for examination. There, many of the "patients" turned out

210

to be high-ranking Nazi garrison officers accompanied by their wives and children.

These unwounded "casualties" were taken ashore, together with their families. The officers, accompanied by the prisoners brought in by *Haida* and *Kelvin,* were routed for a prison camp. As their train pulled out there was a great weeping and wailing from the wives and families behind the wire. Knowing the methods employed by their own people they were certain their husbands and sweethearts were being taken away to be shot.

The grim British guards gave them no comfort or enlightenment.

CONCLUSION

C. in C. will visit H.M.C.S. Haida at 0900 today following which preparations are to be completed for departure and the ship will sail for Halifax, via the Azores, to carry out long refit.

No more nights at Action Stations, no more raiding off the French Coast, no more Murmansk convoys . . . for a time at any rate. Aboard *Haida* a cheerful crew was bustling with activity. Stores and other materials were being loaded for Canada and farewells were being said to those who were being drafted off the ship to bases in England.

A handful of these were R.N. ratings who had been serving in *Haida* for special duty. Others were R.C.N. seamen with British wives who had requested more overseas duty. Also included were several officers and men proceeding on special courses in the British Isles.

Promptly at 0900 hrs. lower decks were cleared and all hands mustered aft on the quarterdeck in their best rig. The big car flying the C. in C.'s flag on the front of the radiator drew up alongside the gangway and, as the pipes shrilled in salute, the Vice Admiral came aboard.

The ship's company regarded him with interest. This was the man who had controlled the destinies of the 10th D.F. since that January day in 1944 when they had first come to this base. He was a seaman, that much was obvious at a glance. His weatherbeaten countenance, curly red hair, craggy eyebrows and sea-washed blue eyes had known the winds of the distant seas. He looked at them, smiled a little and then motioned them to close in around him as he stood on top of a hatch. "Let's not stand on ceremony," he said.

"I have had to work you pretty hard since you joined this

212

Command," he continued. "Often you have come in from sea, tired and looking forward to having some time off, only to find yourselves under fresh sailing orders, though by all usual rights you had earned your liberty.

"It was indeed heartening to me to know that not once, though the demands that were made on you were heavy and onerous, was there the slightest delay, or the slightest slack·ness in carrying these out. It was no pleasure to me to have to make these demands upon you but through it all you have supported me magnificently.

"The requirements of war, the demands on this particular Command, made these conditions necessary. We have had a multitude of things to do and a limited number of ships with which to do them. Here we are in the front line. To us is entrusted the guardianship of the Western Approaches and all that such an important trust involves, including the great convoys and ship movements incidental to the invasion.

"We have kept that trust. Our supply convoys, on which our armies in the field are dependent, have passed daily and nightly through the waters of this Command. They offered to an able enemy, based on the French coast within easy striking distance of these movements, a choice and tremen-dous target totalling close to some six million tons of shipping.

"Up to the present time not a single ton of this vast quantity of shipping has been lost by enemy action in the Plymouth Command. That is a fact of some importance which I feel you will be pleased to know. It will help to make up for the long hours and the ceaseless watch which we have had to maintain.

"So much for the defensive side of our operations. On the offensive side, upon which the defence is based, you and the ships with which you have sailed in company have achieved a similarly fine record.

213

"You have engaged in many fierce and spirited actions in enemy waters, actions in which you have emerged the victors on every occasion. You have bottled up enemy shipping and made the movements of his fighting ships an extremely hazardous operation, even in his own waters.

"In these encounters you have piled up an enviable score. Your Flotilla figures at the moment stand at thirty-four enemy surface ships, including at least three destroyers and many armed escorts, to say nothing of the transports and other craft, definitely sunk; one enemy submarine sunk, and seventeen enemy surface ships, including destroyers, heavily damaged. Of this, you have the lion's share.

"That is only a part of what you have done but it is a part which must give you considerable gratification. It has been achieved with the loss of only one ship, the gallant *Athabaskan*.

"These things show how well you have learned your duty . . . that duty which you have carried out with a courage and coolness that are most commendable. You have displayed a great fighting spirit, coupled with a determination and a persistence which have brought you to victory on every occasion on which you have met and engaged the enemy.

"In the future of men like you, I have every confidence. The qualities which each and every one of you has displayed so abundantly must succeed in bringing you to the fore in any walk of life.

"Here you have made friends, both ashore and afloat. In this old seaport, reputed the worst-blitzed city in Britain, we have, under these wartime conditions, been limited in what we could do for your comfort, but our hearts and our best wishes go with you.

"This is an old port . . . old in history, yet you have shared in making new.history here in our times. I would like to think that you will remember us, as we will remember

214

you, and that you will always have a pleasant recollection of this Command.

"This is not an official speech. It is just a few words between ourselves that I have wanted to say . . . to you who have earned so well every praise which can be given you. Goodbye, Haida, and good-luck!"

Three cheers were called for and they were given with a will, followed by a tiger for the red-headed old seadog who had been their leader. After that, those who could get liberty for an hour or two went off to make their goodbyes, and these included a visit to the graves of those shipmates who had, in the language of the sea, "sailed on their last account", and would rest for evermore in English ground.

Sailing time came and the Captain went up to the Bridge. The lines were slipped smartly and *Haida* swung out into the stream, turned around and got under way down harbour. A little knot of men on the jetty, crew members who had been drafted off, stood there waving goodbye as long as she was in sight.

It was hard to believe that this was the last time in this commission. With that reluctance to leave the things they have come to know, common to those who live in danger, many of the seamen were already looking forward to the time when they would return here again. The sailing was supposed to be very secret but as the ship made her way down past the ferry wharves, little knots of civilians, including many girls, fluttered handkerchiefs in farewell.

"There's Sally," said Joe excitedly. "Her old man and her old lady are with her. See them right beside that bunch of Wrens." Discipline forgotten, he swept his cap off and waved it high in the air.

The Bluenose Killick regarded him indulgently. "You'll be seeing her again soon," he remarked.

215

"You bet," said Joe. "We'll be back here as soon as we finish the refit."

"Get a load of this," said the P.O. of the quarterdeck division, indicating a Wren-manned harbour craft passing close. "It's the Killick's Wren come to say goodbye."

The British girls were standing up and waving to the hands fallen in on deck as they went by. The Bluenose looked long and hard at the coxswain of the boat but did not wave.

"Goodbye Haida. . . . Goodluck!" cried the girls.

"Some secret sailing," commented the Captain dourly, up on the bridge, "The whole place seems to be in on it."

She was round the bend now and passing Drake's Island. Up on Plymouth Hoe were more clusters of fluttering handkerchiefs and arms waving goodbye and then the ship turned seaward on the run down to the Gate, past the buoys of the 10th D.F. and the cruisers.

Ashanti was oiling, but half her length projected beyond the oiler's stern and, as *Haida* passed slowly down, each ship piping her as she passed, it was seen that *Ashanti* had cleared lower decks and all hands were clustered on her quarterdeck and up on X gundeck. As *Haida* came abeam they cheered lustily and heartily and tossed their caps in the air.

It was a moving and memorable tribute. "Gee!" said Joe, "fancy them clearing lower decks for us." Like one man *Haida's* company cheered them back and many eyes were moist with feeling.

Ashanti was a good ship. She had been *Huron's* "chummy-ship" and had extended the same affection to *Haida* after *Huron's* departure. *Ashanti's* crew were a happy, cheerful, likeable crowd. Throughout the long months she had sailed with *Haida*, both ships had fought side by side and they had come to know and appreciate each other as only ships can which have fought in company. To *Ashanti* and

216

her people the R.C.N. Tribals gave full marks. She was a good ship.

Signal lamps were blinking from the destroyers *Ashanti, Blyskawica, Piorun,* and the mighty cruisers *Mauritius* and *Bellona.* Bridge signalmen were working at top speed endeavouring to acknowledge and reply to all the goodwill messages that were pouring in as she steamed steadily seaward.

Haida was between the Gate vessels now, passing through the boom defence nets which protected the harbour. She was sailing out into the dusk of the evening, as had happened so often before, but this time it was a one-way passage. By tomorrow's dawn she would be far to the Westward. She would not be coming back to meet the now well-known hail: "Have you any casualties or survivors?"

The slender column of the Eddystone Light was dead ahead as she turned to starboard down channel. Astern the hands on deck looked aft towards the broad gap between the low hills of Devon which marked the harbour entrance, that old historic harbour which, in their day, this ship's company had come to know so well. As *Haida* made her way Westward it faded gradually into the shadows of the evening over the land.

Round the corner by the great headland of Ushant and South and West to the Azores *Haida* made her swift way. A brief stop in the sun-splashed harbour of Horta and she was Westward bound again. It was farewell to Europe now. No more Murmansk convoys, no more night raids off the French Coast. Eyes and minds were turning towards their own land once again. This ship's company had been a long time away.

"Half-past nine is our E.T.A. (Expected time of arrival) at Halifax and that means the seagate," said a P.O. as he stood with his watch in his hand.

There was a sweepstake on who could forecast most

217

accurately the time of the ship's arrival at the seagate. To avoid duplication, a sufficient number of times, marked off in seconds, had been put in a bag on a day out of England, and each participant had drawn one.

They had come through quite a storm coming up to Cape Sable and it was raining a thin drizzle as they passed Chebucto Head and stood in for the gate.

"She has to be right abeam the gate vessel," called Joe anxiously as they clustered round the watch which had been synchronized with the ship's chronometer. The P.O. was calling the seconds now. "O nine two nine four seven," he said and his finger pressed the stopwatch.

"Twelve seconds early at the gate," he announced. "It's the Killick's sweepstake. He takes the dough." Forthwith he reached for a roll of bills in his pocket and paid them over.

"Oh boy," said Joe, "won't the old Killick take Halifax apart tonight." It was a popular win.

Hands straightened up and the divisions were smartly dressed as they made their way up harbour. Their eyes searched eagerly for the old familiar landmarks. The long Terminal pier was abeam, big enough to dock two Queen Elizabeths. Only a couple of freighters were alongside. A tug was circling out and turning in their wake.

From one of the freighters came the deep roar of her steam whistle; then another one joined in and another and another until every ship in the long harbour seemed to be blowing her whistle. From the tug astern came a sudden splurge of music as a navy brass band struck up *Hearts of Oak*.

Furtively the men looked at each other and then back to the harbour as it slowly dawned on them that this reception was for them. They straightened then and stood very rigidly at attention, a strange look of wonder on their faces. It was their first realization of how the fame of their lean, grim

218

fighting ship had spread across the seas and into the homes throughout Canada.

"I mighta known," said a quartermaster irrelevantly.

"Known what?" asked his mate in a whisper.

"Why my old man wrote. It's the first time he was ever known to write a letter all the time I was away."

"What did he say?"

"He said 'When in the name of God are you fellows going to quit. Every time I pick up a paper you've been at it again.' I'm beginning to understand now."

"Look at the dockyard. Every ship's manned," said the Westerner in an awestruck voice.

It was true. Destroyers, frigates, corvettes, minesweepers, and M.L.'s clustered thick alongside at the piers of the naval dockyard were all manned, their crews lining the rails. Insistent through it all came the continual welcome of hundreds of whistles from ships and some even from ashore. Canada was giving a royal welcome home to her most famous fighting ship.

Slowly *Haida* passed the dockyard. The motor cutter was let go smartly as they went, the ship steaming on towards the Narrows. She would have to enter the Basin and de-ammunition at Bedford Magazine before she could go alongside.

She was passing the Halifax shipyards when across the narrow stretch of water came a sudden burst of cheering from a ship in the drydock.

"It's the Huron!" a seaman shouted in his delight at seeing one of the familiar ships of the Flotilla. "She's cleared lower decks and is cheering us in."

They felt more at home then. *Huron* was here and they would have friends in port. It was still difficult for them to realize they had been accorded the greatest reception ever given a fighting ship in Canada. *Huron's* action touched them deeply. She had been through it just as much as they

219

had yet she was joining enthusiastically in their welcome home. The ship which had cleared lower decks for them as they left Plymouth had been *Huron's* "chummy-ship" *Ashanti,* and now on their arrival in Halifax here was *Huron* herself doing the same thing.

That night they heard a radio broadcast saying they were home. "The crew of the famous H.M.C.S. Haida, the ship whose blazing guns have written a new and imperishable chapter in our country's history, reached Halifax today," said the announcer. "The last time I saw this ship was in the historic harbour of Plymouth, England. She was coming in from sea, scarred and blistered with the marks of battle and her battle ensign was flying at her mast. There were holes from enemy fire through her hull . . . great heaps of empty shell cases lay around her guns and one turret was tilted brokenly over the side . . . but her crew brought her in as cool and unconcerned as if they had been on a routine patrol. I turned and spoke to an English dock-yard matey standing beside me, watching her come in.

" 'Quite a ship,' I said attempting to disguise my pride.

"He looked at me and in his eyes was a scornful astonish-ment at my ignorance. 'That's a great ship, mister,' he said; 'that's the Haida from Canada. She's been in more fights than any other ship in this harbour, and that's saying some-thing. These boys get free beer in every pub in Plymouth tonight and we're proud to give it to them.'

"That was what England thought of them; and now we have them home.

"Think well of what they have done. These are men who were mostly untrained for war, lads from the Maritimes and British Columbia, from Quebec and the prairies, from the villages, towns and cities of Ontario. Many of them had never seen the sea until they came to it in time of war.

220

"In the dark and perilous days when the fate of our country and our Commonwealth hung in the balance, Haida and her sister ships sailed out to face and fight whatever odds might be against them. Neither the ships nor the men who manned them have come through unscathed. They bear the scars of battle and these men have memories that will never be forgotten.

"They did not flinch or fail in the fierce tide of battle. Grim actions took their toll. They saw their shipmates fall, wounded and dying beside them, but with steadfast faith in the justice of their cause they honoured those who fell by fighting on.

"Now they are home, home from the great series of victories which have brought new honours and added new prestige to our arms, home to the land and people from whence they came.

"Take them to your hearts, Canada. This is a great ship which sailed into this old Nova Scotian harbour today, a ship which has earned a great name, a name which will endure forever in our annals of the sea."